I miei occhiali da lettura

President and Publisher Ira Shapiro Executive Vice President Ann Middlebrook Senior Vice President Wendl Kornfeld
Director of Marketing & Sales Karen Hadam Director of Production Zulema Rodriguez
Creative Director Monica Perez Director of Digital Communications Adolfo Vargas

ADVERTISING SALES
Sales Coordinator Randy Puddu Sales Representatives John Bergstrom, Bill Gluth, Jo Ann Miller, Joe Safferson

MARKETING
Marketing Communications Manager Carrie Bloom Marketing Administration Manager Lisa Wilker
Marketing Coordinator Michael McGruder

CREATIVE
Copywriter Tim Doherty Graphic Designer David Deasy Junior Designer Lucie Fernandes

PRODUCTION
Production Manager Chuck Rosenow Production Coordinator Cassandra Cook Production Assistant Martha Jercinovich
Production Administrator Justine Keefe Traffic Assistant Milton Suarez

DIGITAL COMMUNICATIONS & DISTRIBUTION
Digital Communications Coordinator Nathaniel Monsour Book Distribution Coordinator James Kravitz Directory Coordinator Ed Medina

ADMINISTRATION
Controller Brenda Massy Office Manager Janet Higgins Accounts Manager Lesley-Ann Pereira-Hall
Accounting Assistants Mila Livshatz, Michelle Roberts Administrative Assistant Lee Bullock

SPECIAL THANKS TO Juliette Bae, Daniel Corbalis, Hardy T. Hyppolite, Andre Herzegovitch, Helen Kalipetsis,
Kristen Picca, Christina Satriano

US Book Trade Distribution
American Showcase, Inc.
915 Broadway, 14th Floor, New York, New York 10010, Tel 212 673 6600, 800 894 7469
www.showcase.com

For Sales Outside the US
Rotovision S A
Sheridan House, 112/116A, Western Road, HOVE BN3 2AA, England
Tel 44 1273 72 72 68
Fax 44 1273 72 72 69

Service Bureau
The Ace Group, Inc.
Color Separation
Daiichi Systems Graphics Co., Inc. Through PrintPro Ltd., Hong Kong
Printing and Binding
Tien Wah Press (Singapore)
Directory Typesetting
Judi Orlick Design
Published by
American Showcase, Inc.
915 Broadway, 14th Floor, New York, New York 10010
Tel 212 673 6600, 800 894 7469, Fax 212 673 9795
e-mail info@amshow.com, url: www.showcase.com

American Illustration Showcase 21
Book 1 of 2
ISBN 1-887-165-12-6
ISSN 0278-8128

©1998 American Showcase, Inc.
All rights reserved

1

illustration book

american **showcase**

TWENTY-FIRST EDITION

21st edition

COVER CREDITS Front Cover Illustration Matt Manley pages 626, 627 Lead Page Illustration Beppe Giacobbe pages 472, 473

contents

1

illustration book

representatives

representatives

Dedell Inc., Jacqueline (cont.'d)

BUELOW, ALICIA   356, 357

CHAN, RON   336, 337

DAVIS, NANCY   350, 351

FRICHTEL, LINDA   342, 343

GREIF, GENE   358

GRIESBACH/MARTUCCI   359

MILLER, FRANK   352, 353

MILLER, MAX   360, 361

MUNCK, PAULA   354, 355

NACHT, MERLE   340, 341

PARKER, ED   348, 349

SIBTHORP, FLETCHER   334, 335

STUDER, GORDON   344, 345

TUSCHMAN, RICHARD   338, 339

WIGGINS, MICK   330, 331

YOUNGER, HEIDI   364, 365

Dodge, Sharon
SEATTLE, WA   746, 747

BRÜNZ, ROBERT   747

LA PINE, JULIA   746

Foster Artists Representative, Pat
NYC   750, 751

BLAIR, DRU   751

HENDERSON, LOUIS   750

Gatlin Represents, Rita
SAN FRANCISCO, CA   696-701

CHARPENTIER, RUSS   700

HENNESSY, TOM   701

PIRMAN, JOHN   699

ROSS, MARY   696

SHERMAN, WHITNEY   698

VARNEY, DIANE   697

Goldman Agency, David
NYC   774-785

AKGULIAN, NISHAN   783

BARNES, MICHELLE   782

BENDELL, NORM   774, 775

DININNO, STEVE   778, 779

FOX, ROSEMARY   785

NITTA, KAZUSHIGE   784

VARGO, KURT   780, 781

YANG, JAMES   776, 777

Gordon Associates, Barbara
NYC   786-793

AVISHAI, SUSAN   789

CHRISTENSEN, WENDY   793

ELLIOTT, DAVID   790

JAKESEVIC, NENAD   787

JAMES, BILL   786

LAMUT, SONJA   787

SMOLA, JIM   792

STEWART, DON   791

SUH, JOHN   788

Graham Represents, Corey
SAN FRANCISCO, CA   622-632

ANSLEY, FRANK   632

BROOKS, ANDREA   631

CONRAD, JON   628

HARDESTY, DEBRA   630

MANLEY, MATT   626, 627

NAKAMURA, JOEL   629

TILLINGHAST, DAVID   622, 623

ZINGONE, ROBIN   624, 625

Grien, Anita
NYC   795

JOHNSON, JULIE   795

Guenzi Agents, Carol
DENVER, CO   725-731

EMBER, DAVE   726

ERIKSSON, CHRISTER   727

FISHER, MICHAEL   730

I. O. IMAGE   725

KENNEDY, DEAN   729

SULLIVAN, DON   728

WARD, TOM   731

HK Portfolio
NYC   538-551

BROOKS, NAN   542

CARTER, ABBY   543

DAILY, RENÉE   550

DOTY, ELDON   548

EMBER, KATHI   540

GORE, LEONID   539

KENNEDY, ANNE   546

MANDERS, JOHN   538

MEISEL, PAUL   545

O'SHAUGHNESSY, STEPHANIE   549

REED, MIKE   541

SIMARD, RÉMY   551

ULRICH, GEORGE   544

VEROUGSTRAETE, RANDY   547

Hackett, Pat
SEATTLE, WA   796, 797

OCHSNER, DENNIS   796

ROSENWALD, LAURIE   797

Hankins & Tegenborg Ltd.
NYC   688-692

SINOVCIC, MIRO   692

STABIN, VICTOR   688, 689

VAN RYZIN, PETER   690, 691

Hanson, Jim
CHICAGO, IL   798

SMALLISH, CRAIG   798

Hauser, Barb
SAN FRANCISCO, CA   799-801

KRATTER, PAUL   799

PERINI, BEN   800

SALAZAR, MIRO   801

Heflin, Sarah & The Artworks
NYC   552-569

ALLPORT, SOPHIE   562

BIRMINGHAM, CHRISTIAN   556

COHEN, IZHAR   558

COOK, MATTHEW   569

DANN, PENNY   562

DAVIDSON, ANDREW   557

EVERNDEN, GRAHAM   567

HEWGILL, JODY   553

KNOX, CHARLOTTE   568

LAWRENCE, JOHN   568

MALONE, PETER   555

MCCANNON, DESDEMONA   555

MCMENEMY, SARAH   564

MORRIS, ANTON   564

NELSON, ANNIKA   563

PIVEN, HANOCH   554

representatives

POWELL, JENNY 560

SO, MEILO 566

ULRIKSEN, MARK 559

VENTURA, MARCO 565

WOODIN, MARY 560

WORMELL, CHRISTOPHER 561

Holmberg, Irmeli
NYC 610-621

AIZAWA, KAZ 611

BARNES, MELANIE 621

BARSKY, ALEXANDER 614

BELLA, JOSEF 620

BRIDY, DAN 615

COLE, LO 612

DEFREITAS, PETER 617

KELLER, LAURIE 616

KELLEY, BARBARA 610

LANTZ, DAVID 619

LIMER, TINA BELA 618

NELSON, JOHN 620

NIEVES, MEREDITH 621

RIDING, LYNNE 620

SAGONA, MARINA 621

SCHIWALL, LINDA 621

TAGLIANETTI, CLAIRE 620

THACKER, KAT 613

Jett & Associates, Clare
PROSPECT, KY 594-606

BOLTEN, JENNIFER 603

BRAWNER, DAN 598

CABLE, ANNETTE 604

CABLE, MARK 605

CANGEMI, ANTONIO 601

EAGLE, CAMERON 606

FELKER, ROBERT 599

HAMMER, CLAUDIA 602

JONASON, DAVE 597

KIMURA, HIRO 595

MATTOS, JOHN 596

TORP, CYNTHIA 600

WIEMANN, ROY 594

Johnston, Suzy
TORONTO, ON 803-805

LADA, MIR 803

LIAW, ANSON 805

MARTIN, DOUG 804

Kimche, Tania
NYC 807-809

CALDWELL, KIRK 809

MCMILLAN, KEN 808

OLBINSKI, RAFAL 807

Kirchoff/Wohlberg, Inc.
NYC 810, 811

BACKER, MARNI 810

BARNER, BOB 811

DESAIX, DEBORAH 810

GREJNIEC, MICHAEL 811

KIM, JOUNG UN 811

RUTTEN, NICOLE 810

WALLACE, ANDREA 811

Kirsch, Melanie
RHINELANDER, WI 453

KIMBLE, DAVID 453

Korn, Pamela
CANADENSIS, PA 736-739

AJHAR, BRIAN 736, 737

MOORES, JEFF 738, 739

Lavaty, Frank & Jeff
NYC 478-497

ANZALONE, LORI 486, 487

ATTEBERY, CRAIG 492, 493

BERKEY, JOHN 479

D'ANDREA, DOMENICK 491

DELOY, DEE 497

DEMERS, DON 485

DUKE, CHRIS 480, 481

GALLARDO, GERVASIO 478

GENZO, JOHN PAUL 494, 495

HILDEBRANDT, TIM 484

LOGRIPPO, ROBERT 496

OCHAGAVIA, CARLOS 490

SCANLAN, PETER 488, 489

VERKAAIK, BEN 482, 483

Leff Associates, Jerry
NYC 518-537

ACCORNERO, FRANCO 536, 537

CALLANAN, BRIAN 534, 535

CRAWFORD, DENISE 531

GEERINCK, MANUEL 519

HILLIARD, FRED 525

HODGES, MIKE 527

KUNG, LINGTA 522

LE PAUTREMAT, BERTRAND 521

LYNCH, FRED 520

MANNING, MICHELE 530

O'KEEFE, DAVID 526

OLSON, RIK 524

PARISEAU, PIERRE-PAUL 528, 529

PLANK, MICHAEL 523

THELEN, MARY 532, 533

Leighton & Company
BEVERLY, MA 666-673

BOLSTER, ROB 673

BRONSON, LINDA 669

KRAUS, ANNETTE 670

MEEK, STEVE 672

NASH, SCOTT 667

STEIN, AUGUST 671

THERMES, JENNIFER 668

VALERO, ART 666

Lilie, Jim
SAN FRANCISCO, CA 714-719

BOWMAN, ERIC 716, 717

NGUYEN, RICHARD QUAN 719

STERMER, DUGALD 715

TUCKER, EZRA 718

ZIEMIENSKI, DENNIS 714

Lindgren & Smith
NYC 16-53

DUNNICK, REGAN 35

FIEDLER, JOSEPH DANIEL 20

FRASER, DOUG 46, 47

HEINER, JOE & KATHY 52, 53

HYMAN, MILES 21

JACKSON, JEFF 33

JOHNSON, KIM 24

representatives

representatives

FARLEY, MALCOLM 581

FOTY, TOM 577

GARVIE, BEN 580

HARGREAVES, GREG 575

SHEBAN, CHRIS 582

JOHNSON, ISKRA 570, 571

KASUN, MIKE 573

KLAUBA, DOUGLAS 574

KRIZMANIC, TATJANA 578

PETERSON, BRYAN 572

Neis Group, The
SHELBYVILLE, MI 817-821

BOOKWALTER, TOM 819

KIRK, RAINEY 818

LEBARRE, ERIKA 817

LEBARRE, MATT 821

MCLEAN, DON 820

Newborn Group, The
NYC 740, 741

ALLEN, JULIAN 740

CARRUTHERS, ROY 740

FASOLINO, TERESA 741

GIUSTI, ROBERT 740

GOLDSTROM, ROBERT 740

HESS, MARK 741

HOWARD, JOHN H. 741

JUHASZ, VICTOR 740

MARSH, JAMES 741

MCLEAN, WILSON 741

WILCOX, DAVID 741

ZACHAROW, CHRISTOPHER 740

Penny & Stermer Group, The
NYC 822, 823

ELLIS, STEVE 822

STROMOSKI, RICK 823

Potts & Associates, Carolyn
CHICAGO, IL 607-609

BELL, KAREN 608

LAPINE, JULIA 607

VOO, RHONDA 609

Prentice Associates, Vicki
LOS ANGELES, CA 824

VOSS, TOM 824

Rapp, Inc., Gerald & Cullen
NYC 54-131

ADAMS, BETH 54, 55

ANDERSON, PHILIP 56, 57

ASCENCIOS, N. 58, 59

BAKER, GARIN 60, 61

BRIERS, STUART 62, 63

BUSCH, LON 64, 65

DAVIS, JACK 66, 67

DE MICHIELL, ROBERT 68, 69

DOWNS, RICHARD 70, 71

DYNAMIC DUO, THE 72, 73

ENOS, RANDALL 74, 75

FOSTER, PHIL 76, 77

FREDRICKSON, MARK 78, 79

GELB, JACKI 80, 81

GLASS, RANDY 82, 83

HART, THOMAS 84, 85

HOEY, PETER 86, 87

HUGHES, DAVID 88, 89

HULSEY, KEVIN 90, 91

JOHNSON, CELIA 92, 93

KACZMAN, JAMES 94, 95

KELLER, STEVE 96, 97

KING, J.D. 98, 99

KUBINYI, LASZLO 100, 101

LIU, DAVY 102, 103

MAISNER, BERNARD 104, 105

MAYFORTH, HAL 106, 107

MCLIMANS, DAVID 108, 109

MEYEROWITZ, RICK 110, 111

MORSER, BRUCE 112, 113

NAJAKA, MARLIES MERK 114, 115

NORTHEAST, CHRISTIAN 116, 117

O'BRIEN, JAMES 118, 119

ROSENTHAL, MARC 120, 121

SCHUMER, ARLEN 72, 73

SEIFFER, ALISON 122, 123

STEINBERG, JAMES 124, 125

STRUZAN, DREW 126, 127

TRAYNOR, ELIZABETH 128, 129

WITTE, MICHAEL 130, 131

WOLFGANG, SHERRI 72, 73

Ravenhill
KANSAS CITY, MO 825-827

APPLEOFF, SANDY 826

MORDAN, C.B. 827

SKELTON, STEVE 825

Renard Represents
NYC 226-280

BJÖRKMAN, STEVE 252

BOZZINI, JAMES 276

BROOKS, ROB 258, 259

CIGLIANO, BILL 234, 235

DAIGLE, STÉPHAN 272, 273

DONNER, CAROL 277

ELDRIDGE, GARY 236, 237

GARROW, DAN 274, 275

GERAS, AUDRA 278, 279

GROSSMAN, WENDY 238, 239

GUITTEAU, JUD 230, 231

HARRISON, WILLIAM 280

HERBERT, JONATHAN 244, 245

HILL, ROGER 250, 251

HOLMES, MATTHEW 268, 269

MACDONALD, JOHN 254, 255

MARTIN, JOHN 248, 249

MATSU 242, 243

MCGURL, MICHAEL 266, 267

MCLOUGHLIN, WAYNE 253

MILOT, RENÉ 260, 261

MORRIS, JULIE 256, 257

NEWTON, RICHARD 264, 265

PELO, JEFFREY 246, 247

POPE, KEVIN 270, 271

RODRIGUEZ, ROBERT 240, 241

RUDNAK, THEO 232, 233

SANO, KAZUHIKO 227

SINCLAIR, VALERIE 228, 229

SUCHIT, STU 262

WHITESIDES, KIM 263

representatives

Riley Illustration
NYC 752, 753

BENOIT 752

BRAMHALL, WILLIAM 752

DERVAUX, ISABELLE 753

FISHER, JEFFERY 753

GIBBON, REBECCA 752

KOREN, EDWARD 752

LE-TAN, PIERRE 753

LINN, WARREN 752

PYLE, LIZ 753

SHANAHAN, DANNY 753

SIMPSON, GRETCHEN DOW 752

WEISBECKER, PHILIPPE 753

Rogers, Lilla
ARLINGTON, MA 648-657

AZAKAMI, MAKIKO 650

BIGDA, DIANE 649

BOYAJIAN, ANN 654

DE MARCO, KIM 652

FARRINGTON, SUSAN 657

GRAN, ELIZA 653

INGEMANSON, DONNA 651

ROGERS, LILLA 648

SMITH, ANNE 655

WATERS, SUSY PILGRIM 656

S.I. International
NYC 682-687

BAUMANN, KAREN 682

BRACKEN, CAROLYN 682

CARDONA STUDIO 686

CHRISTENSEN, DAVID 685

CK DESIGN 683, 687

COURTNEY, RICHARD 687

CUDDY, ROBBIN 686

DAVIS, ALLEN 686

DURK, JIM 687

EAGLE, BRUCE 682

ENIK, TED 685

GARCIA, SEGUNDO 685

GRANT, MEL 684

GUELL, FERNANDO 682

HANNON, HOLLY 687

HASKAMP, STEVE 686

KENNY, MIKE 687

KUHTIC, CHARES 683

KURISU, JANE 685

KURTZ, JOHN 684

LAPADULA, TOM 682

MARDAROSIAN, MARK 682

MARVIN, FRED 684

MATEU, FRANC 685

MIRALLES, JOSE-MARIA 684

MONES, ISIDRE 683

NINE, CARLOS 686

OSTROM, BOB 683

PICART, GABRIEL 684

RIGOL, FRANCESC 687

RUIZ, ARISTIDES 685

SERRAT-SANS 687

STEVENSON, NANCY 686

THOMPSON BROS. 683

TORRES, JORDI 684

VICENTE, GONZALEZ 685

YEE, JOSIE 687

Sanders Agency, Liz
LAGUNA NIGUEL, CA 828-837

BEE, JOHNEE 833

BOTELHO, CLEMENTE 834

EISLER, SARAH 828

HANTEL, JOHANNA 830

LENSCH, CHRIS 831

LOMELE, BACHRUN 836

NING, AMY 835

REINHARDT, DOROTHY 829

SHAVER, MARK 832

WASSON, CAMERON 837

Seigel, Fran
NYC 366

DEETER, CATHERINE 366

Shannon Associates L.L.C.
NYC 281-327

AKOPYAN, LOUDVIK 282, 283

AUSTIN, CARY 284, 285

BERG, JOHN 286, 287

BOLLINGER, PETER 288-291

BRODNER, STEVE 292, 293

CALL, GREG 294, 295

CARROLL, JIM 296, 297

COWDREY, RICHARD 298, 299

DEVRIES, DAVE 304, 305

DIETZ, MIKE 300, 301

ELLIOTT, MARK 306, 307

ELWELL, TRISTAN 308, 309

FARICY, PATRICK 310, 311

GABOR, TIM 312, 313

HANNA, B. SCOTT 314, 315

JOHNSON, STEPHEN T. 316, 317

KÖELSCH, MICHAEL 318-321

KRAMER, DAVE 322, 323

NIELSEN, CLIFF 324, 325

TORRES, CARLOS 326, 327

WELLES, TOBY 302, 303

Solomon, Richard
NYC 190-225

BARTON, KENT 192, 193

BENNETT, JAMES 194, 195

CLINE, RICHARD 196, 197

COLLIER, JOHN 198, 199

COX, PAUL 200, 201

DAVIS, JACK E. 202, 203

JOHNSON, DAVID 204, 205

KELLEY, GARY 206, 207

KIMBER, MURRAY 208, 209

MANCHESS, GREGORY 210, 211

NELSON, BILL 212, 213

PAYNE, C.F. 214, 215

SMITH, DOUGLAS 216, 217

SUMMERS, MARK 218, 219

URAM, LAUREN 220, 221

VENTURA, ANDREA 222, 223

VERDAGUER, RAYMOND 224, 225

Sweet Represents
SAN FRANCISCO, CA 708-713

COMBS, JONATHAN 708

EVANS, ROBERT 710

representatives

MCCAMPBELL, RACHAEL 711

MUELLER, DEREK 712

NELSON, WILL 709

NOBLE, STEVEN 713

Three In A Box
TORONTO, ONT. 674-681

ADAMS, KATHRYN 676

DALY, BOB 680

FUJIWARA, KIM 675

RITCHIE, SCOT 679

STANLEY, ANNE 678

WATSON, PAUL 674

WHAMOND, DAVE 677

ZGODZINSKI, ROSE 681

Susan and Company
SEATTLE, WA 702-707

EDELSON, WENDY 705

INGRAM, FRED 706

LARSEN, ERIC 707

STADLER, GREG 702, 703

VIBBERT, CAROLYN 704

Tugeau, Christina A.
RIDGEFIELD, CT 838, 839

BERNARDIN, JAMES 839

DAY, LARRY 838

Turk, Melissa & The Artist Network
SUFFERN, NY 633-637

DREW/BROOK/CORMACK ASSOC. 634

LEMONNIER, JOE 633

O'MALLEY, KEVIN 637

SMITH-GRISWOLD, WENDY 635

TAYLOR, BRIDGET STARR 636

Wells, Karen
HOUSTON, TX 693-695

FIRESTONE, BILL 695

MCCORMACK, DAPHNE 693

O'NEIL, SHARRON 694

Wolfe Limited, Deborah
PHILADELPHIA, PA 404-426

BAKER, SKIP 420

BAUER, STEPHEN 412

CAMPBELL, JENNY 406

CANE, LINDA 405

CERICOLA, ANTHONY 407

FITZ-MAURICE, JEFF 424

GNAN, PATRICK 416

HAMBLIN, RANDY 418

HUGHES, MARIANNE 419

KOVACH, JOSEPH PAGE 411

MORROW, J. T. 404

MYER, ANDY 408

NAU, STEVEN 410

PENG, LEIF 425

POMERANTZ, LISA 417

ROMAN, IRENA 423

ROSENBAUM, JONATHAN & GEORGINA 409

ROSENBAUM, SAUL 426

ROSS, SCOTT 422

ROTONDO, NICK 413

WALDREP, RICHARD 414

WINBORG, LARRY 421

WUMMER, AMY 415

EVERY ONE OF OUR ARTISTS IS ON-LINE

STREAMLINED AND INTUITIVE, OUR SITE IS DESIGNED AS A TOOL FOR FINDING TALENT.

A NO-NONSENSE, GET-THE-JOB-DONE TOOL.

THINKING YOU WANT AN ARTIST WHO CREATES COLLAGES?

NEED TO FIND AN ILLUSTRATOR FOR YOUR CHILDREN'S BOOKS?

WISH YOU COULD SEE MORE ART?

OUR WEB SITE WILL HELP YOU DO YOUR JOB.

see
ART

www.showcase.com

WWW.SHOWCASE.COM

At www.showcase.com there are **three** ways to see art.

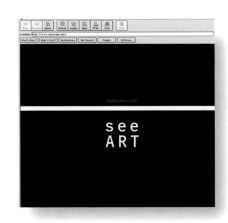

search

Allows you to select specific keywords and hunt for artists according to the subject matter of their imagery, their style, the medium in which they create, and the region where they live.

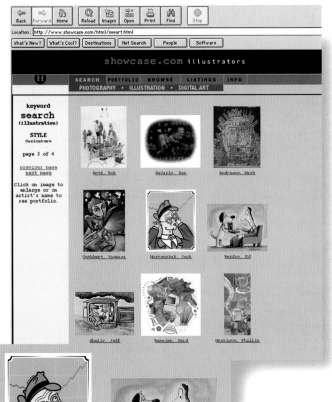

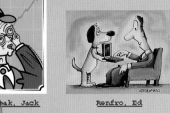

Click on any thumbnail to enlarge.

Click on artist's name to see additional imagery, accessing their portfolio on-line.

WHERE ASSIGNMENT LIVES ON-LINE

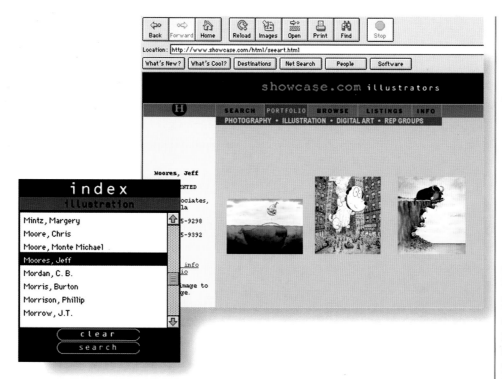

portfolio

Lets you access artists' portfolios directly. Or you can sample the work of all the artists handled by a particular Representative.

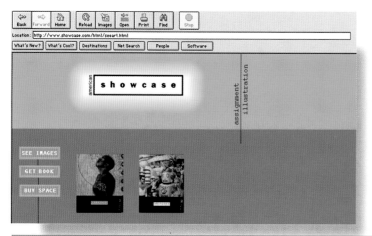

browse

Presents a random selection of imagery from Showcase Illustration advertisers.

listings Provides complete contact information for all artists.

steven salerno

lindgren & smith

representatives > patricia lindgren / piper smith / tricia weber
new york 212.397.7330 / www.lindgrensmith.com / san francisco 415.788.8552

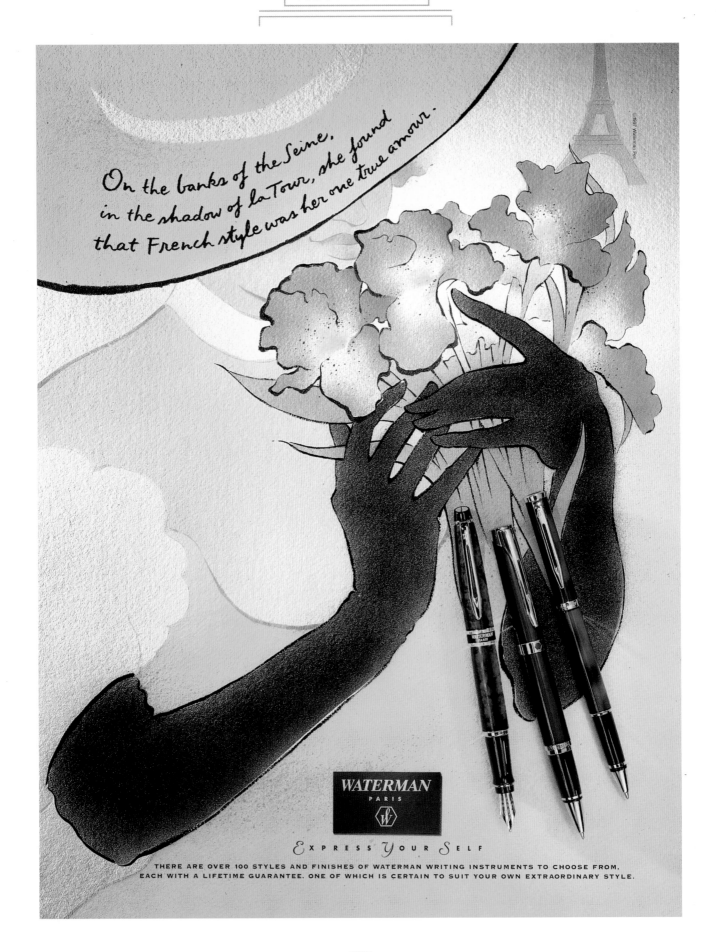

lindgren & smith

representatives ➤ patricia lindgren / piper smith / tricia weber
new york 212.397.7330 / www.lindgrensmith.com / san francisco 415.788.8552

22

lindgren & smith

representatives > patricia lindgren / piper smith / tricia weber
new york 212.397.7330 / www.lindgrensmith.com / san francisco 415.788.8552

lindgren & smith

representatives › patricia lindgren / piper smith / tricia weber
new york 212.397.7330 / www.lindgrensmith.com / san francisco 415.788.8552

32

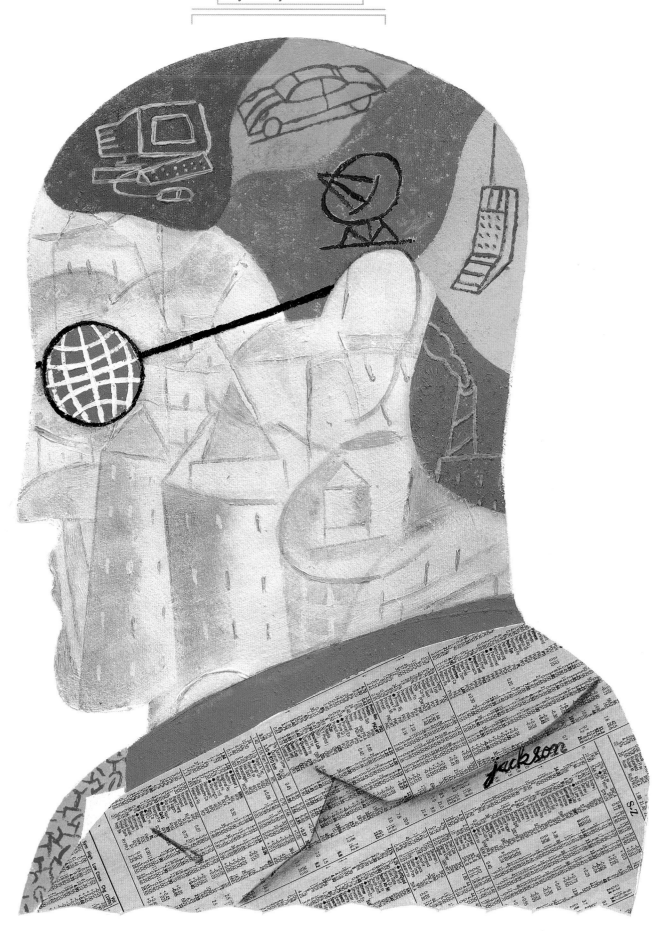

lindgren & smith

representatives > patricia lindgren / piper smith / tricia weber
new york 212.397.7330 / www.lindgrensmith.com / san francisco 415.788.8552

   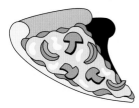 

lindgren & smith

representatives › patricia lindgren / piper smith / tricia weber
new york 212.397.7330 / www.lindgrensmith.com / san francisco 415.788.8552

ILLustration AND
Really Dumb Pie charts

regan dunnick

TRIKES BY COLOR

ALIEN ABDUCTION OF COWS BY REGION

PATTY'S PIE FILLIN'

SALES IN MILWAUKEE

Percentage of Dogs who catch FRISBEES

High Finance stuff

lindgren & smith

representatives > patricia lindgren / piper smith / tricia weber
new york 212.397.7330 / www.lindgrensmith.com / san francisco 415.788.8552

DAD MAKES THINGS

lindgren & smith

representatives › patricia lindgren / piper smith / tricia weber
new york 212.397.7330 / www.lindgrensmith.com / san francisco 415.788.8552

lindgren & smith

representatives › patricia lindgren / piper smith / tricia weber
new york 212.397.7330 / www.lindgrensmith.com / san francisco 415.788.8552

lindgren & smith

representatives > patricia lindgren / piper smith / tricia weber
new york 212.397.7330 / www.lindgrensmith.com / san francisco 415.788.8552

lindgren & smith

representatives > patricia lindgren / piper smith / tricia weber
new york 212.397.7330 / www.lindgrensmith.com / san francisco 415.788.8552

lindgren & smith

representatives › patricia lindgren / piper smith / tricia weber
new york 212.397.7330 / www.lindgrensmith.com / san francisco 415.788.8552

lindgren & smith

representatives › patricia lindgren / piper smith / tricia weber
new york 212.397.7330 / www.lindgrensmith.com / san francisco 415.788.8552

lindgren & smith

representatives > patricia lindgren / piper smith / tricia weber
new york 212.397.7330 / www.lindgrensmith.com / san francisco 415.788.8552

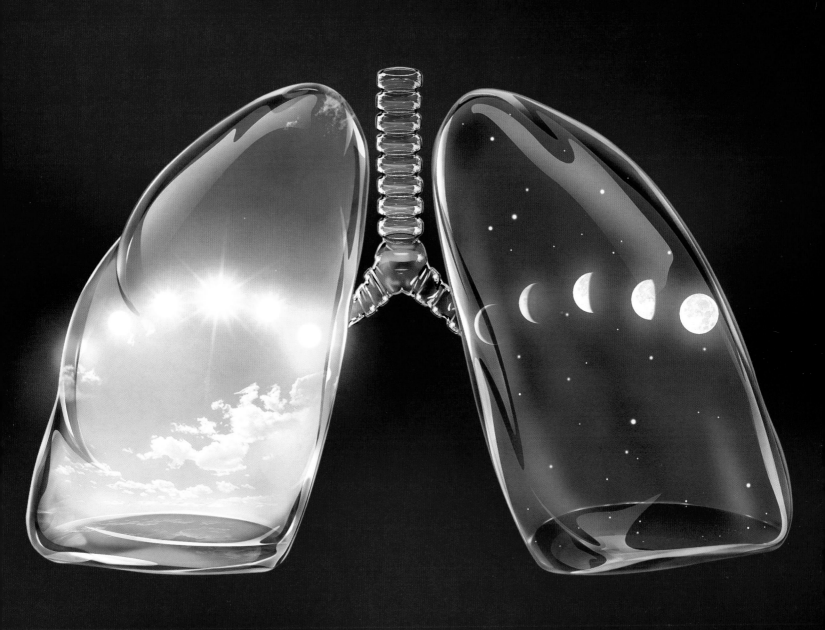

Beth Adams

Gerald & Cullen Rapp, Inc.
108 E. 35th St. N.Y., N.Y. 10016
PH: 212 987 8700
fax: 212 889 3341
www.theispot.com/artist/adams

Shortbread
30 sweet+savory recipes

by JANN JOHNSON
illustrations by BETH ADAMS

Beth Adams

Gerald & Cullen Rapp, Inc.
108 E. 35th St. N.Y., N.Y. 10016
PH: 212 987 8700
fax: 212 889 3341
www.theispot.com/artist/adams

Philip Anderson

Gerald & Cullen Rapp, Inc.
108 East 35 St., New York, NY 10016
Ph: (212) 889-3337 Fax (212) 889-3341
www.theispot.com/artist/anderson

Philip ANDERSON

Philip Anderson

Gerald & Cullen Rapp, Inc.
108 East 35 St., New York, NY 10016
Ph: (212) 889-3337 Fax (212) 889-3341
www.theispot.com/artist/anderson

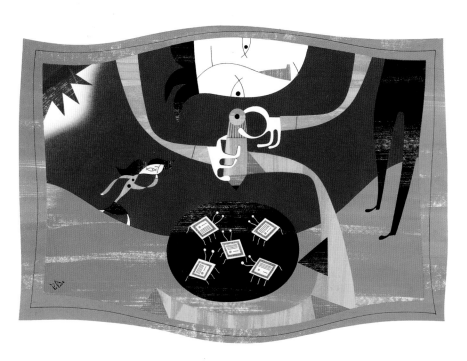

PHILIP ANDERSON

Garin Baker

Gerald & Cullen Rapp, Inc.
108 East 35 St., New York, NY 10016
Ph: (212) 889-3337 Fax (212) 889-3341
www.theispot.com/artist/baker

Garin Baker

Gerald & Cullen Rapp, Inc.
108 East 35 St., New York, NY 10016
Ph: (212) 889-3337 Fax (212) 889-3341
www.theispot.com/artist/baker

Gerald & Cullen Rapp, Inc.
108 East 35 St., New York, NY 10016
Ph: (212) 889-3337 Fax (212) 889-3341
www.theispot.com/artist/briers

Stuart Briers

Gerald & Cullen Rapp, Inc.
108 East 35 St., New York, NY 10016
Ph: (212) 889-3337 Fax (212) 889-3341
www.theispot.com/artist/briers

Lon Busch

Gerald & Cullen Rapp, Inc.
108 East 35 St., New York, NY 10016
Ph: (212) 889-3337 Fax (212) 889-3341
www.theispot.com/artist/busch

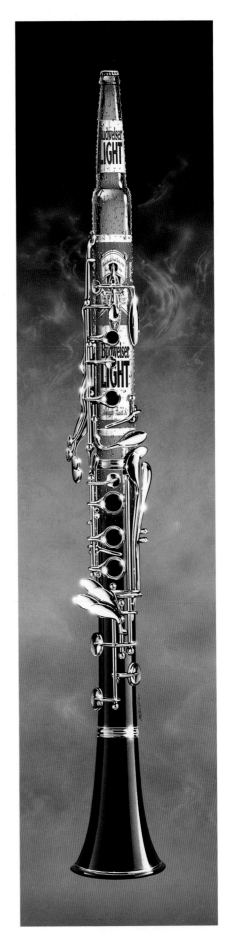

Lon Busch

Gerald & Cullen Rapp, Inc.
108 East 35 St., New York, NY 10016
Ph: (212) 889-3337 Fax (212) 889-3341
www.theispot.com/artist/busch

Gerald & Cullen Rapp, Inc.
108 East 35 St., New York, NY 10016
Ph: (212) 889-3337 Fax (212) 889-3341
www.theispot.com/artist/davis

Jack Davis

Gerald & Cullen Rapp, Inc.
108 East 35 St., New York, NY 10016
Ph: (212) 889-3337 Fax (212) 889-3341
www.theispot.com/artist/davis

Gerald & Cullen Rapp, Inc.
108 East 35 Street
New York, New York 10016
tel: 212 889 3337   fax: 212 889 3341
www.theispot.com/artist/demichiell

Robert de Michiell

Gerald & Cullen Rapp, Inc.
108 East 35 Street
New York, New York 10016
tel: 212 889 3337 fax: 212 889 3341
www.theispot.com/artist/demichiell

Robert de Michiell

Richard Downs

Gerald & Cullen Rapp, Inc.
108 East 35 St., New York, NY 10016
Ph: (212) 889-3337 Fax (212) 889-3341
www.theispot.com/artist/downs

Richard Downs

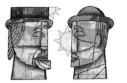

Gerald & Cullen Rapp, Inc.
108 East 35 St., New York, NY 10016
Ph: (212) 889-3337 Fax (212) 889-3341
www.theispot.com/artist/downs

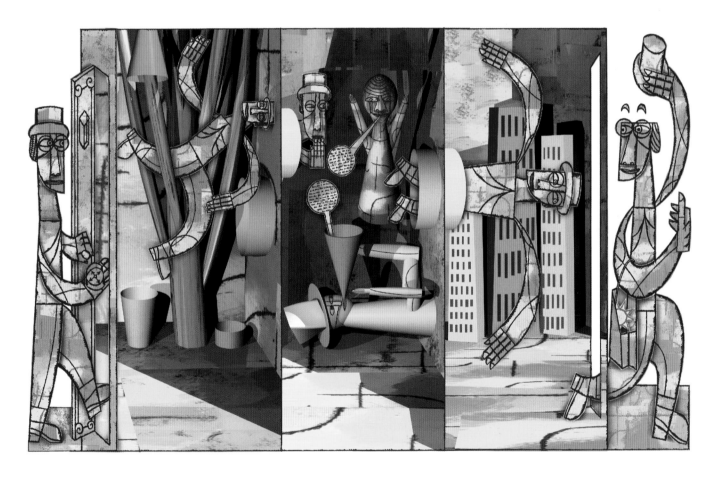

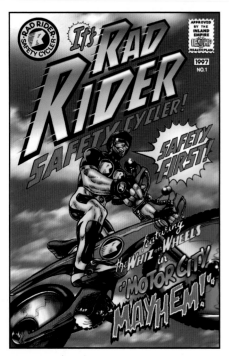

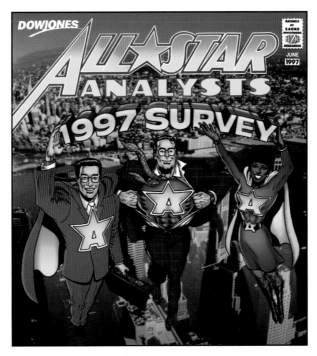

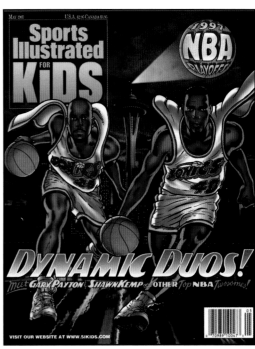

The DYNAMIC DUO®

ARLEN SCHUMER & SHERRI WOLFGANG

REPRESENTED BY

GERALD & CULLEN RAPP, INC.

108 East 35 St.
New York 10016
Phone: (212) 889-3337
Fax: (212) 889-3341

Randall Enos

Gerald & Cullen Rapp, Inc.
108 East 35 St., New York, NY 10016
Ph: (212) 889-3337 Fax (212) 889-3341
www.theispot.com/artist/enos

Randall Enos

Gerald & Cullen Rapp, Inc.
108 East 35 St., New York, NY 10016
Ph: (212) 889-3337 Fax (212) 889-3341
www.theispot.com/artist/enos

PHIL FOSTER

Gerald & Cullen Rapp, Inc.
108 East 35 St., New York, NY 10016
Ph: (212) 889-3337 Fax (212) 889-3341
www.theispot.com/artist/foster

PHIL FOSTER

Gerald & Cullen Rapp, Inc.
108 East 35 St., New York, NY 10016
Ph: (212) 889-3337 Fax (212) 889-3341
www.theispot.com/artist/foster

Mark Fredrickson

Gerald & Cullen Rapp, Inc.
108 East 35 St., New York, NY 10016
Ph: (212) 889-3337 Fax (212) 889-3341
www.theispot.com/artist/fredrickson

Mark Fredrickson

Gerald & Cullen Rapp, Inc.
108 East 35 St., New York, NY 10016
Ph: (212) 889-3337 Fax (212) 889-3341
www.theispot.com/artist/fredrickson

jacki Gelb

eats spoonfuls of bee pollen

Gerald & Cullen Rapp, Inc.
108 East 35 St., New York, NY 10016
Ph: (212) 889-3337 Fax (212) 889-3341
www.theispot.com/artist/gelb

JACKi GELb

Gerald & Cullen Rapp, Inc.
108 East 35 St., New York, NY 10016
Ph: (212) 889-3337   Fax (212) 889-3341
www.theispot.com/artist/gelb

Randy Glass

Gerald & Cullen Rapp, Inc.
108 East 35 St., New York, NY 10016
Ph: (212) 889-3337 Fax (212) 889-3341
www.theispot.com/artist/glass

Randy Glass

Gerald & Cullen Rapp, Inc.
108 East 35 St., New York, NY 10016
Ph: (212) 889-3337 Fax (212) 889-3341
www.theispot.com/artist/glass

How to turn your coffee

into

FAT FREE

delicious coffeehouse cappuccino.

Make your own delicious cappuccino right in your own home. No fuss, no mess, no fat.

Carnation® Coffee-mate® Cappucino Creamers

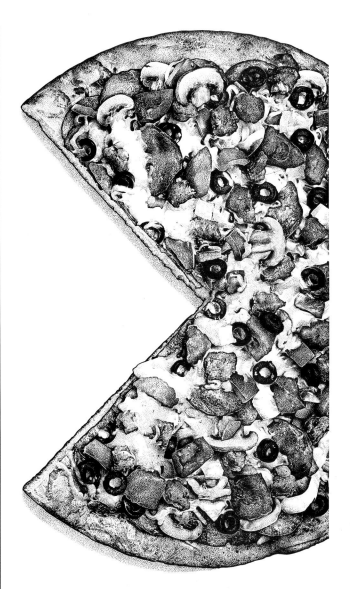

SAVINGS OF AMERICA

ESTABLISHED 1889

RAPP ART

GERALD & CULLEN RAPP · THOMAS HART
№ 212 889-3337 108 EAST 35th ST. NYC 10016
FAX 212 889-3341

NOW IS THE TIME 1997

Dr Pepper

THIS IS THE PLACE

THIS IS THE TASTE

marketing

Party with the Stone.

oh, I Come Frum Argentinaaa wit a sitar on my kneeeeee

THOMAS HART

TBS
NBA
THURSDAY

NOV 10 MAGIC @ KNICKS
NOV 17 BULLS @ ROCKETS
JAN 14 WARRIORS @ PACERS
NOV 24 SUNS @ BULLS
DEC 8   ROCKETS @ ROCKETS
DEC 15 NUGGETS @ HEAT
DEC 29 SUNS @ ROCKETS
DEC 29 MAGIC @ HORNETS
JAN 5   SPURS @ JAZZ
JAN 12 HEAT @ SPURS
JAN 19 KNICKS @ ROCKETS
JAN 26 BULLS @ MAGIC
FEB 2   SUPERSONICS @ MAGIC
FEB 9   WARRIORS @ NUGGETS
FEB 16 ROCKETS @ HORNETS
FEB 23 76ERS @ NUGGETS
MAR 2   BULLS @ KNICKS GAME 1
MAR 9   MAGIC @ ROCKETS GAME 2
MAR 16 SPURS @ CAVALIERS
MAR 23 SUNS @ HORNETS
MAR 30 HORNETS @ MAGIC
APR 6   HAWKS @ SPURS
APR 13 SUPERSONICS @ MAGIC
APR 20 WARRIORS @ JAZZ
APR 27 KNICKS @ NUGGETS

Thursday Nights just got BIGGER

TBS

stormy WEATHER

We State the Obvious:

PETER HOEY is *represented by* GERALD AND CULLEN RAPP INC.
108 E. 35th St. New York, NY, 10016
phone: 212. 889. 3337 *fax:* 212. 889. 3341
online portfolio: www.theispot.com/artist/hoey

YIPPEE

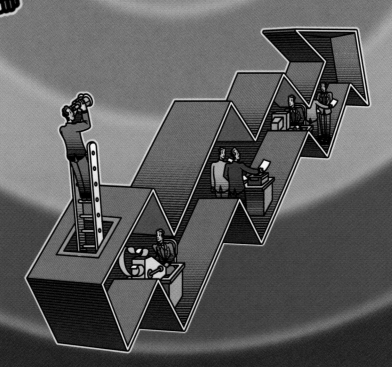

David Hughes

Gerald & Cullen Rapp, Inc.
108 East 35 St., New York, NY 10016
Ph: (212) 889-3337   Fax (212) 889-3341

David Hughes

Gerald & Cullen Rapp, Inc.
108 East 35 St., New York, NY 10016
Ph: (212) 889-3337 Fax (212) 889-3341

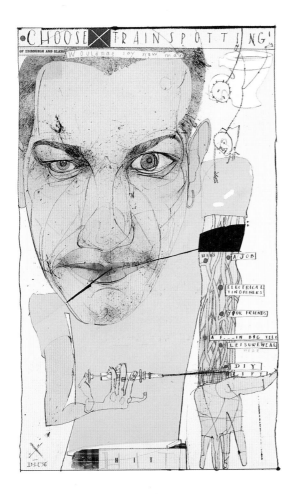

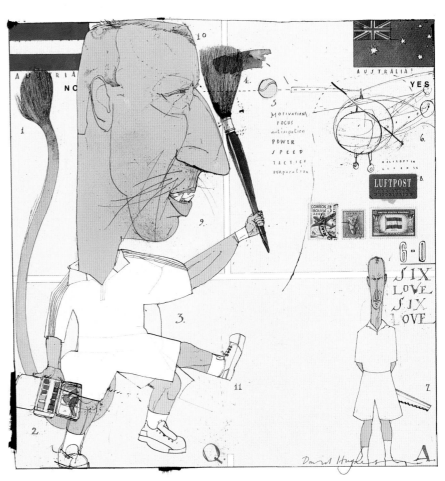

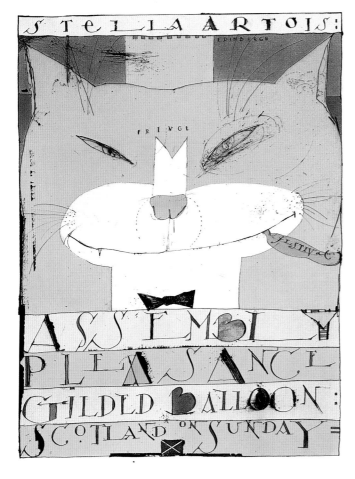

Kevin Hulsey

Gerald & Cullen Rapp, Inc.
108 East 35 St., New York, NY 10016
Ph: (212) 889-3337 Fax (212) 889-3341

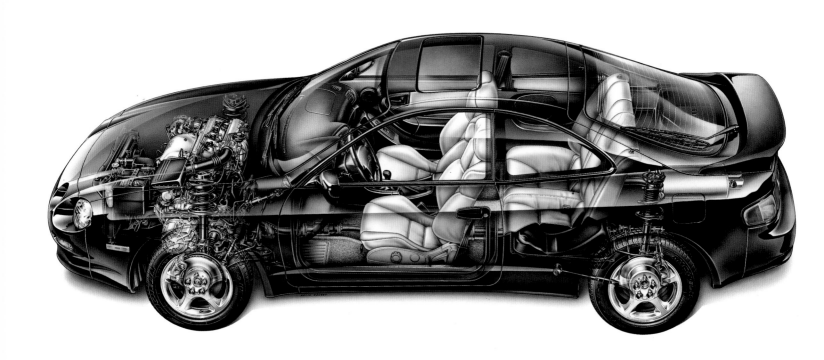

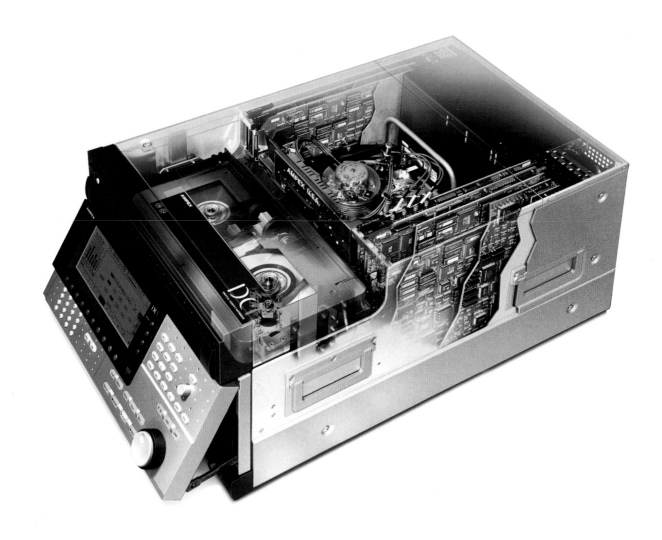

Kevin Hulsey

Gerald & Cullen Rapp, Inc.
108 East 35 St., New York, NY 10016
Ph: (212) 889-3337 Fax (212) 889-3341

GERALD & CULLEN RAPP, INC.

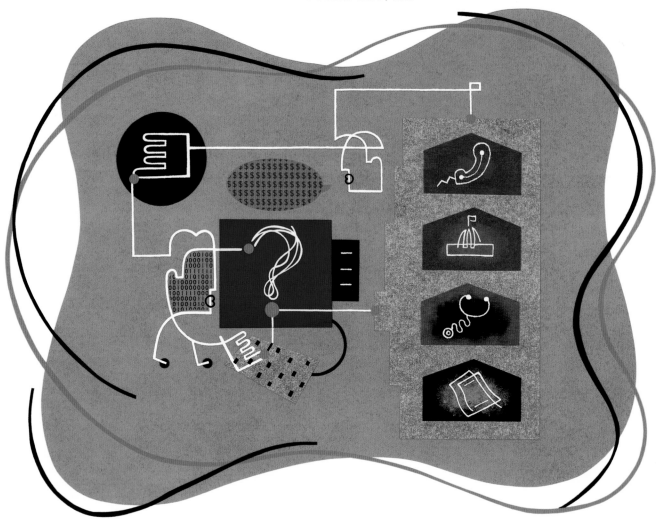

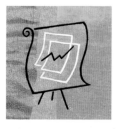

JAMES KACZMAN

GERALD & CULLEN RAPP, INC.
108 EAST 35 ST., NEW YORK, NY 10016
PH: 212 889 3337 FAX: 212 889 3341
WWW.THEISPOT.COM/ARTIST/KACZMAN

Steve Keller

Gerald & Cullen Rapp, Inc.
108 East 35 St., New York, NY 10016
Ph: (212) 889-3337 Fax (212) 889-3341
www.theispot.com/artist/keller

teve Keller

Gerald & Cullen Rapp, Inc.
108 East 35 St., New York, NY 10016
Ph: (212) 889-3337 Fax (212) 889-3341
www.theispot.com/artist/keller

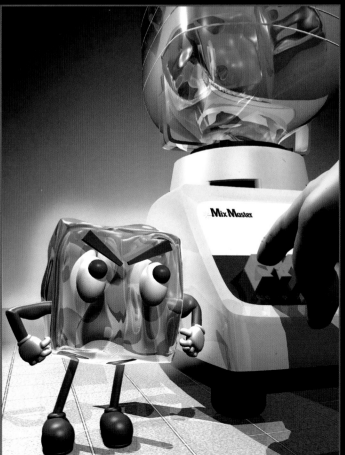

Gerald & Cullen Rapp, Inc.

108 East 35th Street
New York, NY 10016
Phone: (212) 889-3337
Fax: (212) 889-3341
www.theispot.com/artist/king

New York Magazine

VISA Card

Nick at Nite

New York Magazine

J.D.KING

Gerald & Cullen Rapp, Inc.
Phone: (212) 889-3337

Tower PULSE

Laszlo Kubinyi

Gerald & Cullen Rapp, Inc.
108 East 35 St., New York, NY 10016
Ph: (212) 889-3337 Fax (212) 889-3341
www.theispot.com/artist/kubinyi

THE WALL STREET JOURNAL AMERICAS.

CIRCULATION

Country	Paper	Circulation
ARGENTINA	LA NACIÓN	197,000
BOLIVIA	HOY	20,000
BRAZIL	ESTADO DE MINAS	89,000
BRAZIL	JORNAL DO BRASIL	120,000
BRAZIL	O ESTADO DE S. PAULO	350,000
CHILE	EL MERCURIO	112,000
COLOMBIA	EL TIEMPO	264,000
COSTA RICA	LA NACIÓN	107,078
DOMINICAN REPUBLIC	LISTÍN DIARIO	85,000
ECUADOR	EL COMERCIO	100,000
EL SALVADOR	LA PRENSA GRÁFICA	109,423
GUATEMALA	SIGLO VEINTIUNO	54,000
HONDURAS	LA PRENSA	46,000
MEXICO	REFORMA	100,000
NICARAGUA	LA PRENSA	39,000
PANAMA	LA PRENSA	36,000
PERU	EL COMERCIO	120,000
URUGUAY	EL PAÍS	45,000
VENEZUELA	EL NACIONAL	120,000

THE WALL STREET JOURNAL AMERICAS
TOTAL CIRCULATION   2,104,501

Laszlo Kubinyi

Gerald & Cullen Rapp, Inc.
108 East 35 St., New York, NY 10016
Ph: (212) 889-3337 Fax (212) 889-3341
www.theispot.com/artist/kubinyi

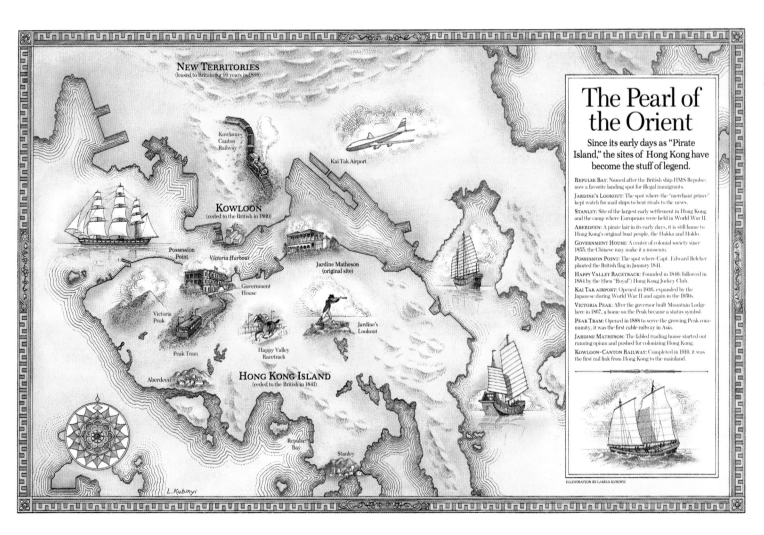

Davy Liu

Gerald & Cullen Rapp, Inc.
108 East 35 St., New York, NY 10016
Ph: (212) 889-3337 Fax (212) 889-3341
www.theispot.com/artist/liu

Davy Liu

Gerald & Cullen Rapp, Inc.
108 East 35 St., New York, NY 10016
Ph: (212) 889-3337 Fax (212) 889-3341
www.theispot.com/artist/liu

BERNARD MAISNER - HAND LETTERING

Gerald & Cullen Rapp, Inc. 108 E. 35th St., NYC 10016 Ph:(212) 889-3337 Fx:(212) 889-3341 e-mail:BMaisner@aol.com

BERNARD MAISNER
"CONJURER OF LETTERFORMS"

PHOTO: MONICA STEVENSON

HAL Mayforth

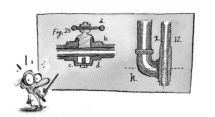

GERALD & CULLEN RAPP, INC.
108 E. 35TH ST. NY, NY 10016
P: 212·889·3337 F: 212·889·3341
www.theispot.com/artist/mayforth

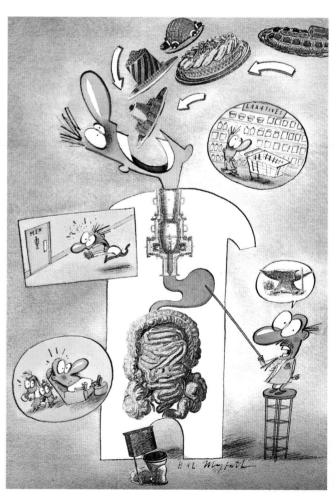

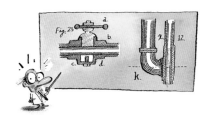

HAL Mayforth

GERALD & CULLEN RAPP, INC.
108 E. 35TH ST. NY, NY 10016
P: 212-889-3337 F: 212-889-3341
www.theispot.com/artist/mayforth

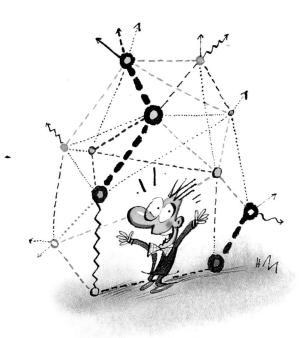

David McLimans

Gerald & Cullen Rapp, Inc.
108 East 35 St., New York, NY 10016
Ph: (212) 889-3337 Fax (212) 889-3341
www.theispot.com/artist/mclimans

David McLimans

Gerald & Cullen Rapp, Inc.
108 East 35 St., New York, NY 10016
Ph: (212) 889-3337 Fax (212) 889-3341
www.theispot.com/artist/mclimans

Rick Meyerowitz

GERALD & CULLEN RAPP, INC.
108 EAST 35TH ST. NEW YORK, NY. 10016
PHONE (212) 889-3337
FAX (212) 889-3341
WWW.theispot.com/artist/meyerowitz

Bruce Morser

Gerald & Cullen Rapp, Inc.
108 East 35 St., New York, NY 10016
Ph: (212) 889-3337 Fax (212) 889-3341
www.theispot.com/artist/morser

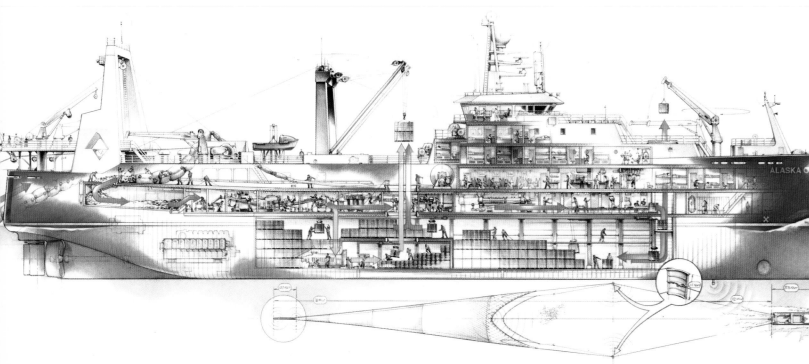

Bruce Morser

Gerald & Cullen Rapp, Inc.
108 East 35 St., New York, NY 10016
Ph: (212) 889-3337 Fax (212) 889-3341
www.theispot.com/artist/morser

Marlies Merk Najaka

Gerald & Cullen Rapp, Inc.
108 East 35 St., New York, NY 10016
Ph: (212) 889-3337 Fax (212) 889-3341
www.theispot.com/artist/najaka

Marlies Merk Najaka

Gerald & Cullen Rapp, Inc.
108 East 35 St., New York, NY 10016
Ph: (212) 889-3337 Fax (212) 889-3341
www.theispot.com/artist/najaka

Marlies Merk Najaka

CHRISTIAN NORTHEAST

Gerald & Cullen Rapp,Inc. Ph:(212)889-3337 Fax(212)889-3341 www.theispot.com/artist/northeast

CHRISTIAN NORTHEAST

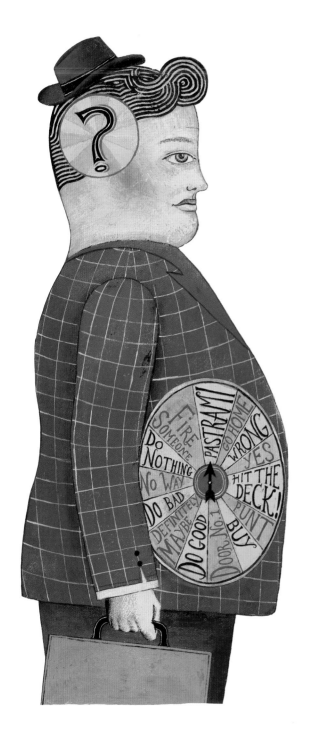

James O'Brien

Gerald & Cullen Rapp, Inc.
108 East 35 St., New York, NY 10016
Ph: (212) 889-3337 Fax (212) 889-3341
www.theispot.com/artist/o'brien

James O'Brien

Gerald & Cullen Rapp, Inc.
108 East 35 St., New York, NY 10016
Ph: (212) 889-3337 Fax (212) 889-3341
www.theispot.com/artist/o'brien

Alison Seiffer

Gerald & Cullen Rapp, Inc.
108 East 35 St., New York, NY 10016
Ph: (212) 889-3337 Fax (212) 889-3341
www.theispot.com/artist/seiffer

Alison Seiffer

Gerald & Cullen Rapp, Inc.
108 East 35 St., New York, NY 10016
Ph: (212) 889-3337 Fax (212) 889-3341
www.theispot.com/artist/seiffer

James Steinberg

Gerald & Cullen Rapp, Inc.
108 East 35 St., New York, NY 10016
Ph: (212) 889-3337 Fax (212) 889-3341
www.theispot.com/artist/steinberg

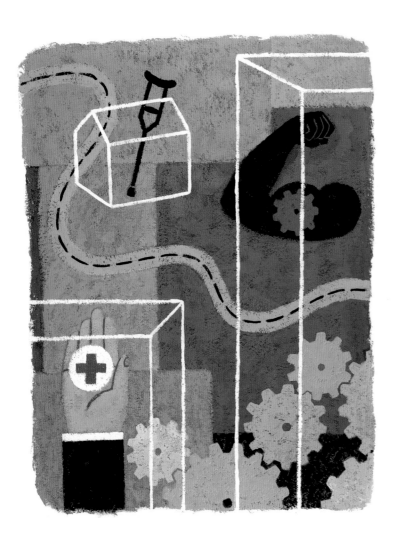

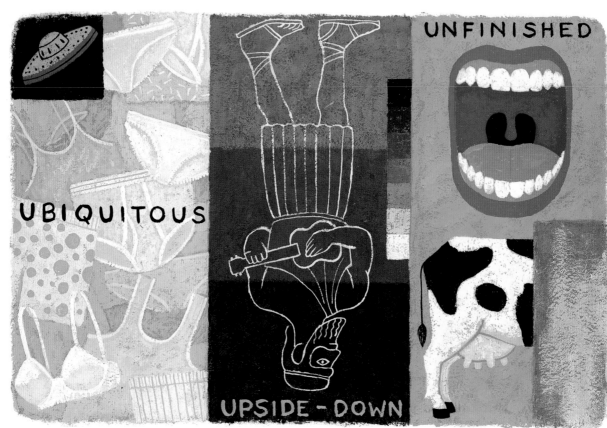

James Steinberg

Gerald & Cullen Rapp, Inc.
108 East 35 St., New York, NY 10016
Ph: (212) 889-3337 Fax (212) 889-3341
www.theispot.com/artist/steinberg

Dear George,

Congratulations for renewing the most enduring motion picture in cinema history.

Elizabeth
Traynor

Gerald & Cullen Rapp, Inc.
108 East 35 St., New York, NY 10016
Ph: (212) 889-3337 Fax (212) 889-3341
www.theispot.com/artist/traynor

128

Elizabeth Traynor

Gerald & Cullen Rapp, Inc.
108 East 35 St., New York, NY 10016
Ph: (212) 889-3337 Fax (212) 889-3341
www.theispot.com/artist/traynor

UNDERGROUND atlanta ™

HUNTERS GLEN
The Villages of Marlborough

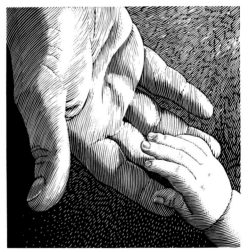

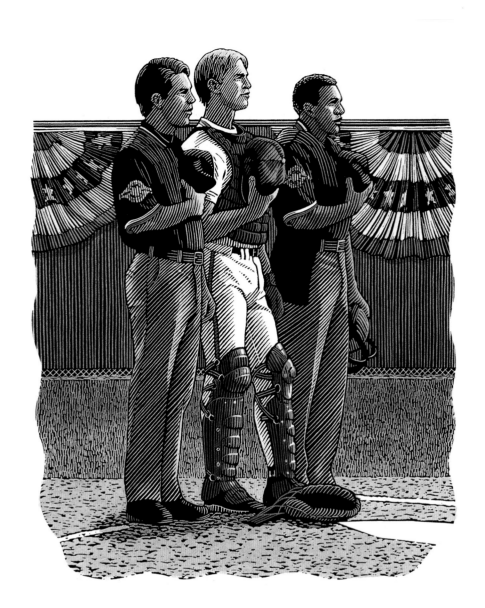

sunkist

Michael Witte

Gerald & Cullen Rapp, Inc.
108 East 35 St., New York, NY 10016
Ph: (212) 889-3337 Fax (212) 889-3341
www.theispot.com/artist/witte

Michael Witte

Gerald & Cullen Rapp, Inc.
108 East 35 St., New York, NY 10016
Ph: (212) 889-3337 Fax (212) 889-3341
www.theispot.com/artist/witte

Mendola LTD.

ARTIST REPRESENTATIVES

420 LEXINGTON AVE. NEW YORK N.Y. 10170

212•986•5680

WWW.MENDOLAART.COM

FAX 212•818•1246

MANGIAT

CORNERS

RESENTATIVES
. NEW YORK N.Y. 10170
86·5680
WWW.MENDOLAART.COM

Mendola LTD.

WAYNE VINCENT

DDB Needham Chicago

Paul Tsang Design

Randomsoft • Design by Woods + Woods

Saifman Richards

Major League Baseball

MENDOLA LTD.
212-986-5680
www.mendolaart.com

EDITORIAL
703-532-8551
wvassoc@aol.com

WAYNE VINCENT

Better Homes and Gardens®

New JUNIOR Cookbook

Meredith Corp.

HELLO!

MENDOLA LTD.
212-986-5680
WWW.MENDOLAART.COM

EDITORIAL
703-532-8551
WVASSOC@AOL.COM

To see more illustrations, icons and cool typographic elements call MENDOLA, or check out my website...

Russell Benfanti
www.benfanti.com

Sam Ward

MENDOLA LTD.
ARTISTS REPRESENTATIVES
212 **986-5680** FAX 212 818-1246
420 LEXINGTON AVE. NEW YORK, N.Y. 10170

Editorial 703 256-8313

Sam Ward

MENDOLA LTD.
ARTISTS REPRESENTATIVES
212 **986-5680** FAX 212 818-1246
420 LEXINGTON AVE. NEW YORK, N.Y. 10170

Editorial 703 256-8313

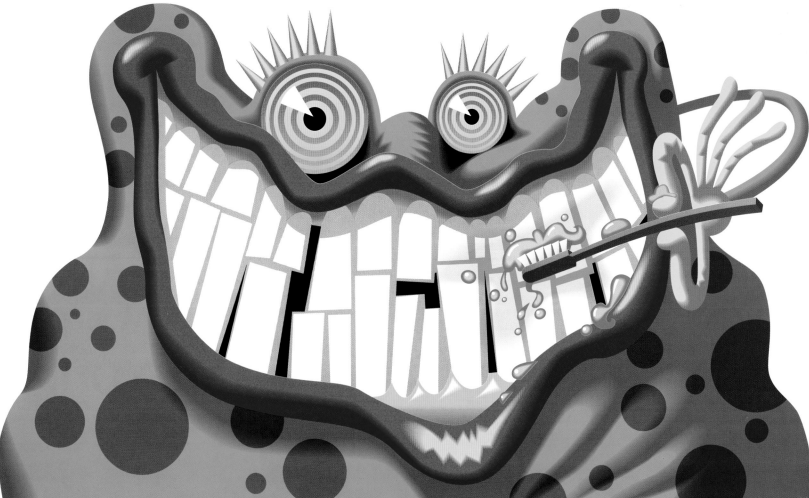

FRANCESCO
SANTALUCIA

ROWAN BARNES~MURPHY

Mendola Ltd. Graybar Bldg. 420 Lexington Ave. Penthouse. New York. N.Y. 10170
Tel. 212 986 5680 ~ FAX 212 818 1246
See His on Line Portfolio at www.MendolaArt.com.

MICHAEL
CRAMPTON

MICHAEL
CRAMPTON

146

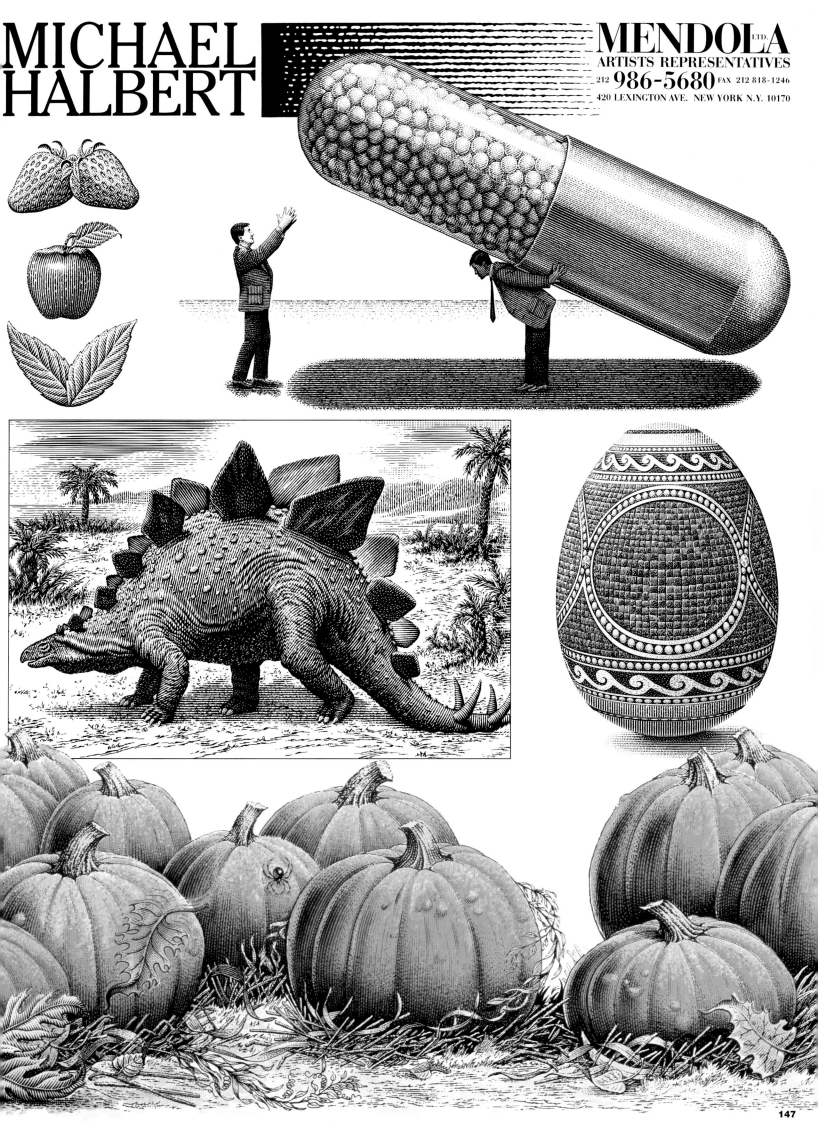

MICHAEL HALBERT

MENDOLA LTD.
ARTISTS REPRESENTATIVES
212 986-5680 FAX 212 818-1246
420 LEXINGTON AVE. NEW YORK N.Y. 10170

CORNEL RUBINO

MENDOLA LTD
Artists Representatives
420 Lexington Avenue
New York, NY 10170
212 986.5680 T
212 818.1246 F

3 Ring Circus

Goldilocks And The 3 Bears

3 Men In A Tub

CORNEL RUBINO

MENDOLA LTD
Artists Representatives
420 Lexington Avenue
New York, NY 10170
212 986.5680 T
212 818.1246 F

WATERCOLOR AND INK

Chezem
Doug Chezem

WESTERN UNION®

PREFERRED CUSTOMER

TICKETMASTER
THE ENTERTAINMENT CARD

Money

1972-1997
25 YEAR
ANNIVERSARY

MENDOLA
ARTIST'S REPRESENTATIVES
212986-5680
FAX 212 818-1246
420 LEXINGTON AVE,
NEW YORK, NY 10170
Editorial 703-591-5424

SEE THE ONLINE PORTFOLIO AT
www.mendolaart.com

MENDOLA LTD.
ARTISTS REPRESENTATIVES
212 **986-5680** FAX 212 818-1246
420 LEXINGTON AVE. NEW YORK N.Y. 10170
Portfolio Online @ www.MendolaArt.com

editorial 212-242-4319

Rudolph, Rein of Terror

McCann-Erickson

TOM NEWSOM

DAVID HENDERSON

156

MIKE WIMMER-I DO ART INC.

3905 NICOLE CIRCLE, NORMAN, OK 73072, 405-329-0478

"He's knocked another one out of the park!"

Robert Tanenbaum

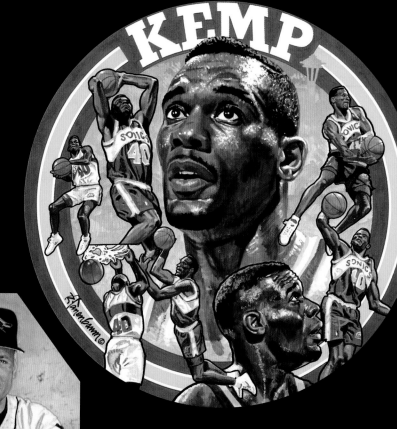

STEVEN CHORNEY

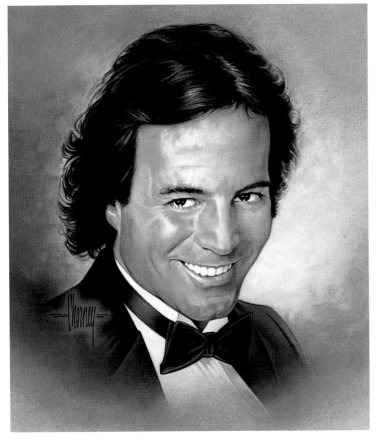

JASON DOWD

Long Lasting Freshness

April Fresh

Downy

25 SINGLE SHEETS

25 6.75 x 12 IN. SHEETS (17.1 x 30.4 cm)

NOTARILE

ILLUSTRATOR

PRIMESTAR

PROGRAM GUIDE · NOVEMBER 1996

$3.50

Tune In As PRIMESTAR® Serves Up
2 New Channels
of TV Stars for
Thanksgiving!

COMEDY CENTRAL

Nick at Nite's
TV LAND

SEE PAGE 2

NBA Season Opens
Story on page 7

Tyson vs. Holyfield
NOVEMBER 9TH
See Inside Back Cover For Details

Stuff yourself on all
this Thanksgiving. Details

2 New Channels at
No Additional Charge! Story

Only OREO
1912 85th ANNIVERSARY EDITION 1997

FOR SANTA
YOUR
FAVORITE
COOKIES

NET WT 16 OZ (1LB)

1997

THE AMERICAN
BENEFACTOR

SUMMER 1997

Will You
Help?

RON BERG
Illustration

Jim Talbot

13 DEAD END DRIVE

Ages 9 and Up

2 to 4 Players

The Butler

The Maid

The Chauffeur

The Cat

MB.
Milton Bradley

The Mystery Game with 12 Suspects, 5 Traps and Only 1 Survivor!

MILK & Cookies

ELECTRONIC
M-M-MOOOOS
TELL YOU WHERE
THE MILK IS!

Molly MooCow's
Cookie Dunking Game

AGES 4 AND UP
PARKER BROTHERS

DON WIELAND

ROBERT HYNES

KITCHELL

Go Fish!

Go Wild!

Go

ROBERT MONDAVI

Coastal

MENDOLA LTD.
ARTISTS REPRESENTATIVES
212 **986-5680** FAX 212 818-1246
420 LEXINGTON AVE. NEW YORK N.Y. 10170

DENISE & FERNANDO

ED MARTINEZ

DEAN WILLIAMS

ATTILA HEJJA

GARRY COLBY

COLBY 97 ©

The MousePad

Gillie Schattner

Represented by: Mendola Ltd~
Tel:212.986.5680   Fax:212.818.1246
420 Lexington Ave. New York N.Y. 10170

JONATHAN MILNE · PAPER SCULPTURE

David Schleinkofer

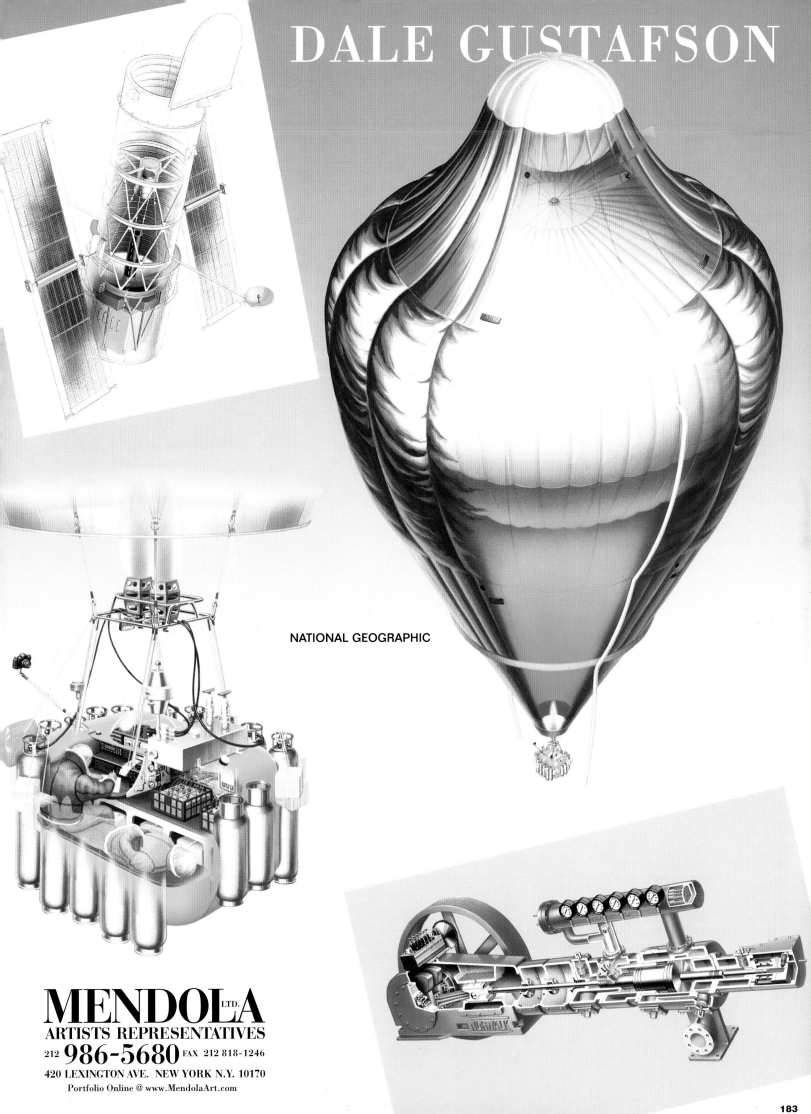

DALE GUSTAFSON

NATIONAL GEOGRAPHIC

LARRY WINBORG

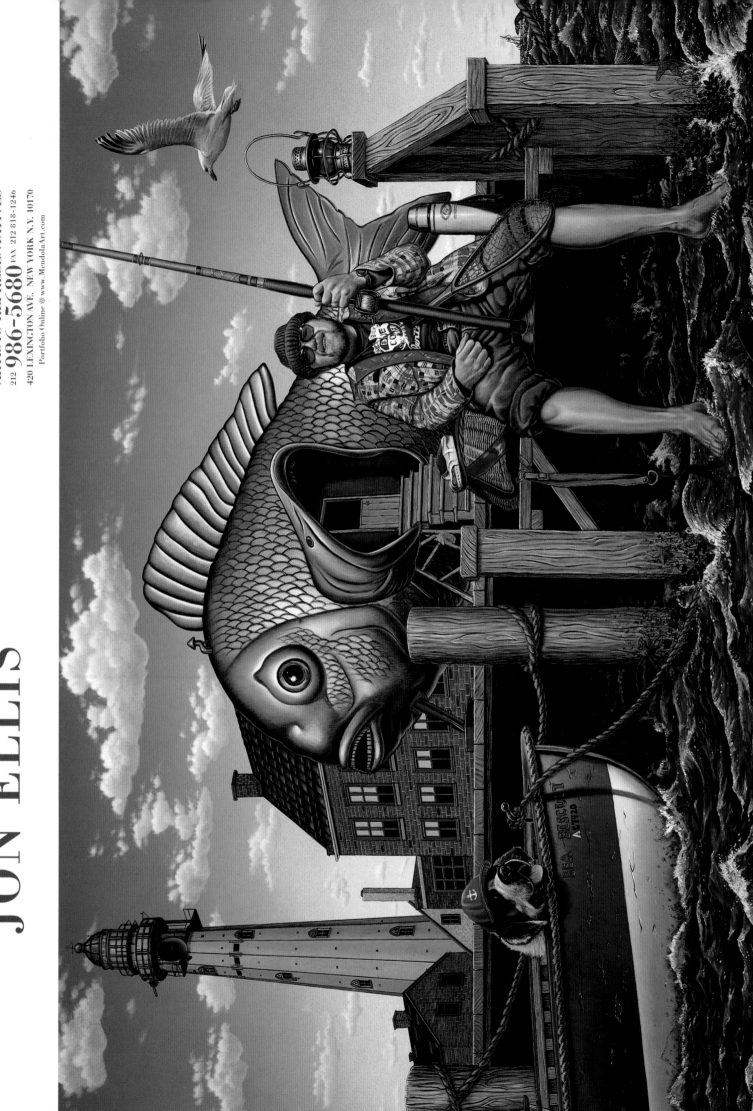

HEY DiDDle DIDDLE THE cat AND THE FiDDLE

The COW JUMPED over the MOON

the LiTTLE Dog LAUGHED to see SUCH CRAFT

and The DiSh s Ran Away WitH the SPOON

amy L. WASSERMAN COLLAGE iLLUSTRATiON
REPRESENTED BY MENDOLA ARTiSTS
PHONE 212-986-5680

Fax 212-818-1246

Inspired by "La Femme Nikita"

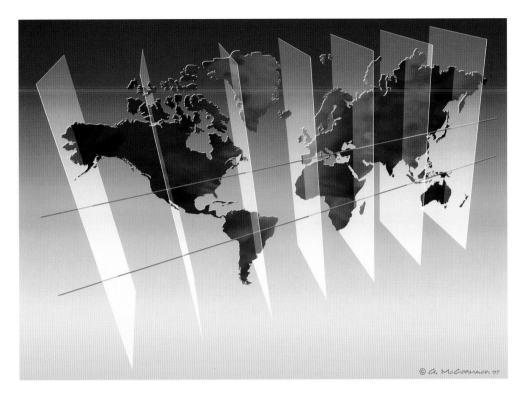

Geoffrey McCormack

DIGITAL ILLUSTRATION
e-mail • mccormac@harborside.com

KENT BARTON · JAMES BENNETT

RICHARD CLINE · JOHN COLLIER

PAUL COX · JACK E. DAVIS

DAVID JOHNSON · GARY KELLEY

MURRAY KIMBER · GREGORY

RICHARD

MANCHESS · BILL NELSON

C.F. PAYNE · DOUGLAS SMITH

MARK SUMMERS · LAUREN URAM

ANDREA VENTURA · RAYMOND VERDAGUER

SOLOMON

THE RUGGED BAJA SHIRT/SCRATCHBOARD & WATERCOLOR

RICHARD SOLOMON
ARTIST REPRESENTATIVE

1 2 1   M A D I S O N   A V E   N Y C   1 0 0 1 6 (2 1 2)   6 8 3 - 1 3 6 2   F A X :   (2 1 2)   6 8 3 - 1 9 1 9

DUSTIN HOFFMAN & SEAN CONNERY IN "FAMILY BUSINESS"/SCRATCHBOARD

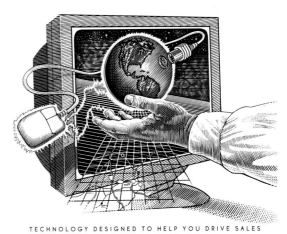

TECHNOLOGY DESIGNED TO HELP YOU DRIVE SALES

KISS ME DEADLY

RICHARD SOLOMON
ARTIST REPRESENTATIVE

21 MADISON AVE NYC 10016 (212) 683-1362 FAX: (212) 683-1919

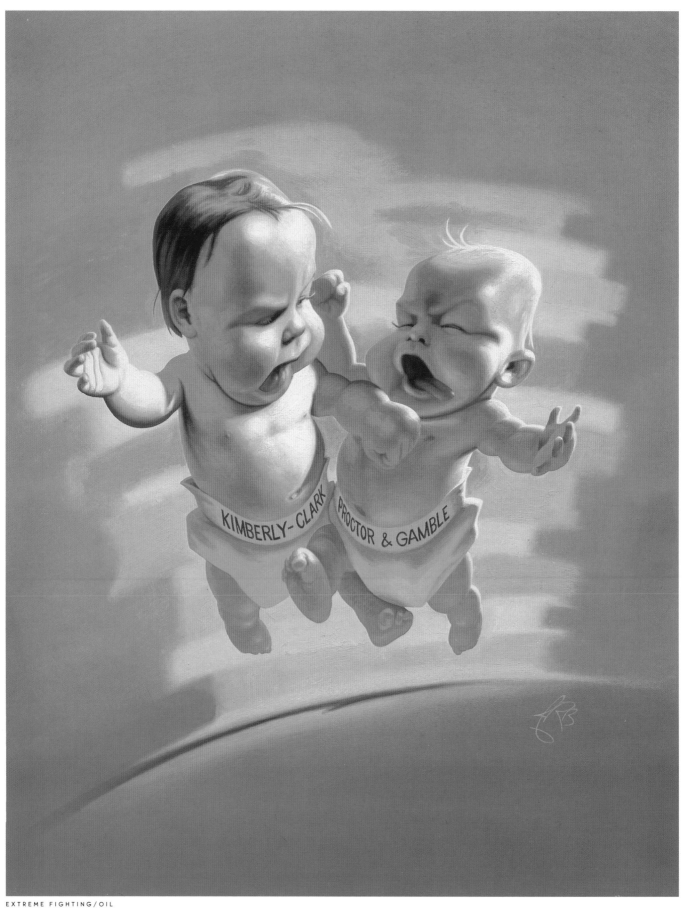

EXTREME FIGHTING/OIL

RICHARD SOLOMON
ARTIST REPRESENTATIVE

121 MADISON AVE NYC 10016 (212) 683-1362 FAX: (212) 683-191

JAMES BENNETT

TIGER WOODS/OIL

CORPORATE COACHING

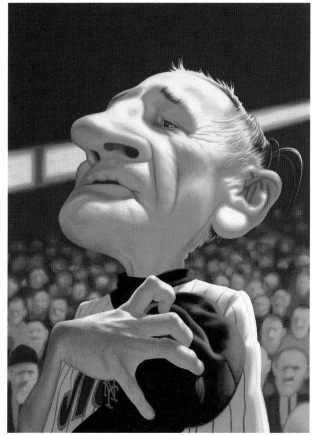

CASEY STENGEL: THE OL' PROFESSOR

MONICA SELES

RICHARD SOLOMON
ARTIST REPRESENTATIVE

121 MADISON AVE NYC 10016   (212) 683-1362 FAX: (212) 683-1919

"Men are like umbrellas, sooner or later, you leave them in bars."

RICHARD SOLOMON
ARTIST REPRESENTATIVE

121 MADISON AVE NYC 10016 (212) 683-1362 FAX: (212) 683-1919

"*Actions speak louder than words, on the other hand, cash screams.*"

RICHARD SOLOMON
ARTIST REPRESENTATIVE

121 MADISON AVE NYC 10016 (212) 683-1362 FAX: (212) 683-1919

JOHN COLLIER

PECONIC BAY / PASTEL

WHEN WE WERE YOUNG

FIRST BLOOM / MONOPRINT

RICHARD SOLOMON
ARTIST REPRESENTATIVE

121 MADISON AVE NYC 10016 (212) 683-1362 FAX: (212) 683-1919

DESTINY BECKONS/PASTEL

RICHARD SOLOMON
ARTIST REPRESENTATIVE

121 MADISON AVE NYC 10016 (212) 683-1362 FAX: (212) 683-1919

BABY, DREAM YOUR DREAM/WATERCOLOR

PAUL COX

THE SHADOW OF YOUR SMILE / WATERCOLOR

RICHARD SOLOMON
ARTIST REPRESENTATIVE

121 MADISON AVE NYC 10016 (212) 683-1362 FAX: (212) 683-1919

JACK E. DAVIS

THE MANHATTAN PROJECT/COLORED PENCIL

RICHARD SOLOMON
ARTIST REPRESENTATIVE

121 MADISON AVE NYC 10016 (212) 683-1362 FAX: (212) 683-1919

JACK E. DAVIS

DOWNSIZING/COLORED PENCIL

RICHARD SOLOMON
ARTIST REPRESENTATIVE

121 MADISON AVE NYC 10016 (212) 683-1362 FAX: (212) 683-1919

DAVID JOHNSON

WOOSTER & JEEVES/P.G. WODEHOUSE/PEN & INK

RICHARD SOLOMON
ARTIST REPRESENTATIVE

1 2 1   M A D I S O N   A V E   N Y C   1 0 0 1 6 (2 1 2)   6 8 3 - 1 3 6 2   F A X :   (2 1 2)   6 8 3 - 1 9 1 •

W.B. YEATS/INK & WATERCOLOR

BERNARD MALAMUD

GALLANT'S ADVENTURE

ROBERT WASHINGTON, JR.: LEGAL SHARK

R I C H A R D   S O L O M O N
A R T I S T   R E P R E S E N T A T I V E

1 2 1   M A D I S O N   A V E   N Y C   1 0 0 1 6   (212) 683-1362   FAX: (212) 683-1919

THE COTTON CLUB/PASTEL

RICHARD SOLOMON
ARTIST REPRESENTATIVE

121 MADISON AVE NYC 10016 (212) 683-1362 FAX: (212) 683-191

GARY KELLEY

THE MUSE/PASTEL

CHELSEA MORNING

MURRAY KIMBER

THE RETOOLING OF RUSSIA/OIL

RICHARD SOLOMON
ARTIST REPRESENTATIVE

121 MADISON AVE NYC 10016 (212) 683-1362 FAX: (212) 683-1919

WORKERS' SYMPHONY/OIL

TAKING IN THE CATCH

DREW BLEDSOE OF THE NEW ENGLAND PATRIOTS/OIL

RICHARD SOLOMON
ARTIST REPRESENTATIVE

ROUSTABOUTS HAUL PIPE IN HEAVY WEATHER/OIL

THE CHASE

RENT/COLORED PENCIL

RICHARD SOLOMON
ARTIST REPRESENTATIVE

121 MADISON AVE NYC 10016 (212) 683-1362 FAX: (212) 683-1919

LITTLE SHOP OF HORRORS/COLORED PENCIL

OUR LITTLE DUTCHBOY

GOH CHOK TONG: PRIME MINISTER OF SINGAPORE

RICHARD SOLOMON
ARTIST REPRESENTATIVE

C.F. PAYNE

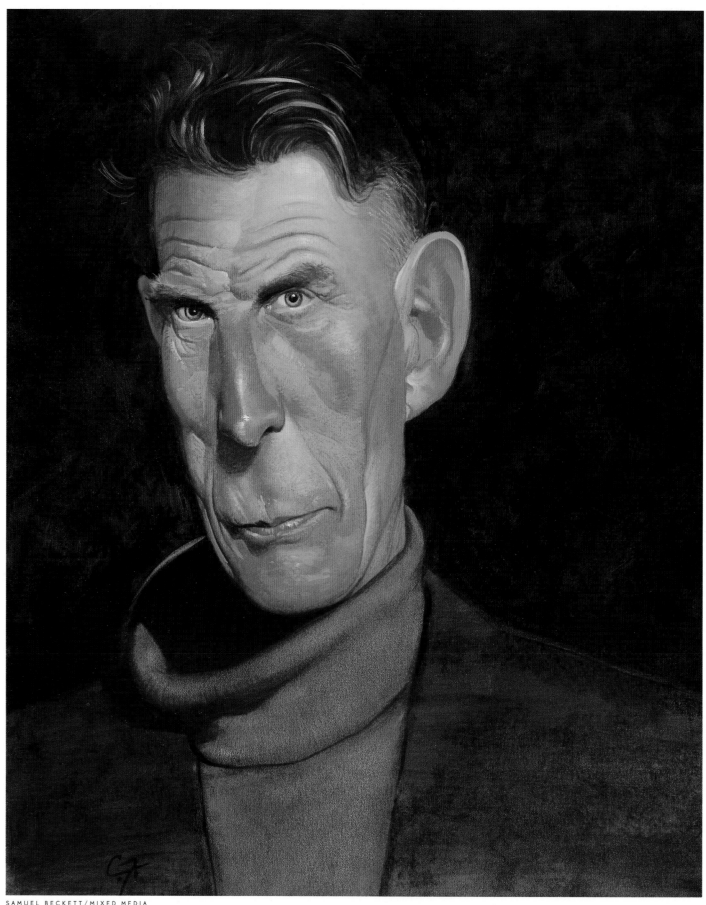

SAMUEL BECKETT / MIXED MEDIA

RICHARD SOLOMON
ARTIST REPRESENTATIVE

121 MADISON AVE NYC 10016 (212) 683-1362 FAX: (212) 683-1919

DEAD MAN TALKING/MIXED MEDIA

JACKIE ROBINSON

THE INS AND OUTS OF SAME-SEX WEDDINGS

WASTING TIME ON-LINE

RICHARD SOLOMON
ARTIST REPRESENTATIVE

DOUGLAS SMITH

THE VENERABLE DOW GETS A MAKEOVER/SCRATCHBOARD & WATERCOLOR

RICHARD SOLOMON
ARTIST REPRESENTATIVE

121 MADISON AVE NYC 10016   (212) 683-1362 FAX: (212) 683-1919

DOUGLAS SMITH

THE GAZEBO/SCRATCHBOARD

WINGS OF PRINT

THE ARBORIST

RICHARD SOLOMON
ARTIST REPRESENTATIVE

121 MADISON AVE NYC 10016 (212) 683-1362 FAX: (212) 683-1919

EDWARD VII
(1841-1910)

WATERCOLOR & ENGRAVING IN SCRATCHBOARD

RICHARD SOLOMON
ARTIST REPRESENTATIVE

121 MADISON AVE NYC 10016 (212) 683-1362 FAX: (212) 683-1919

MARK SUMMERS

THINK INTENTLY AND SPEND WISELY

UNCLE SAM WANTS YOU

LOGO/WELLS FARGO/ENGRAVING IN SCRATCHBOARD

RICHARD SOLOMON
ARTIST REPRESENTATIVE

121 MADISON AVE NYC 10016 (212) 683-1362 FAX: (212) 683-1919

TIGER WOODS: SPORTSMAN OF THE YEAR/PAPER COLLAGE

RICHARD SOLOMON
ARTIST REPRESENTATIVE

121 MADISON AVE NYC 10016 (212) 683-1362 FAX: (212) 683-1919

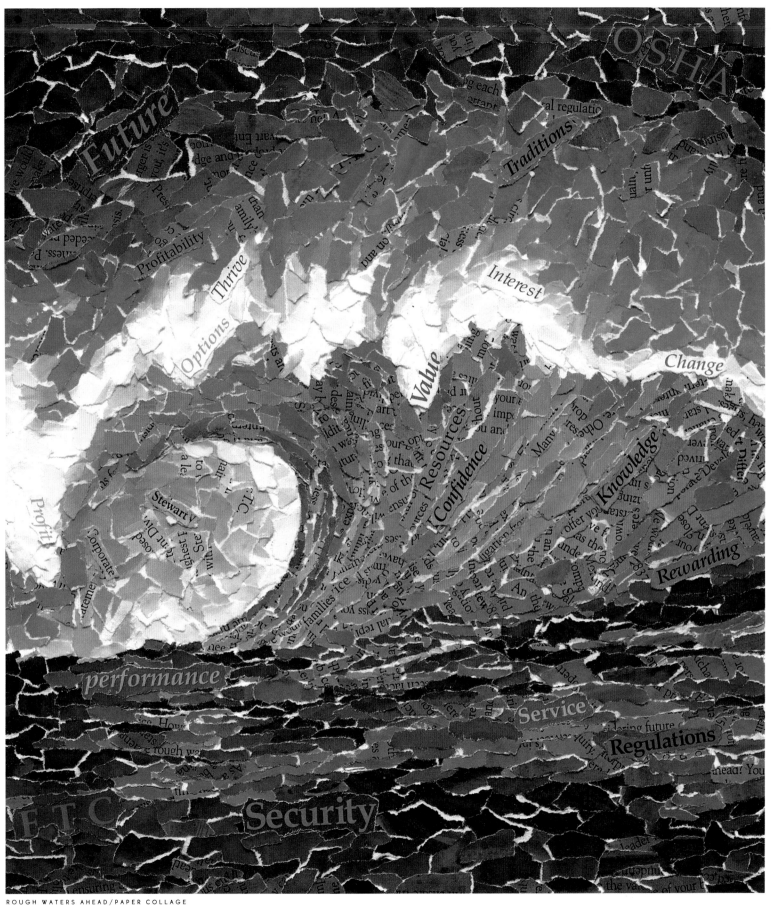

ROUGH WATERS AHEAD / PAPER COLLAGE

RICHARD SOLOMON
ARTIST REPRESENTATIVE

21 MADISON AVE NYC 10016 (212) 683-1362 FAX: (212) 683-1919

BERLIN ALEXANDERPLATZ/ALFRED DÖBLIN/MIXED MEDIA

RICHARD SOLOMON
ARTIST REPRESENTATIVE

121 MADISON AVE NYC 10016 (212) 683-1362 FAX: (212) 683-191

CHARLES DE GAULLE/MIXED MEDIA

ALFRED HITCHCOCK

DAVID STAROBIN

PRAMOEDYA ANANTA TOER

RICHARD SOLOMON
ARTIST REPRESENTATIVE

21 MADISON AVE NYC 10016 (212) 683-1362 FAX: (212) 683-1919

BIG CATS WORK OUT/LINOLEUM CUT

RICHARD SOLOMON
ARTIST REPRESENTATIVE

121 MADISON AVE NYC 10016 (212) 683-1362 FAX: (212) 683-1919

RAYMOND VERDAGUER

MIDSUMMER NIGHT SWING / MULTICOLORED LINOLEUM CUT

RICHARD SOLOMON
ARTIST REPRESENTATIVE

121 MADISON AVE NYC 10016 (212) 683-1362 FAX: (212) 683-1919

225

RENARD

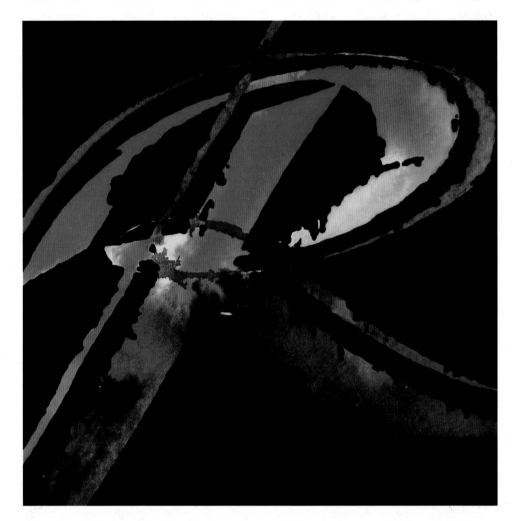

REPRESENTS

TEL: 212-490-2450 • FAX: 212-697-6828 • www.renardrepresents.com
501 FIFTH AVENUE, NEW YORK, NY 10017

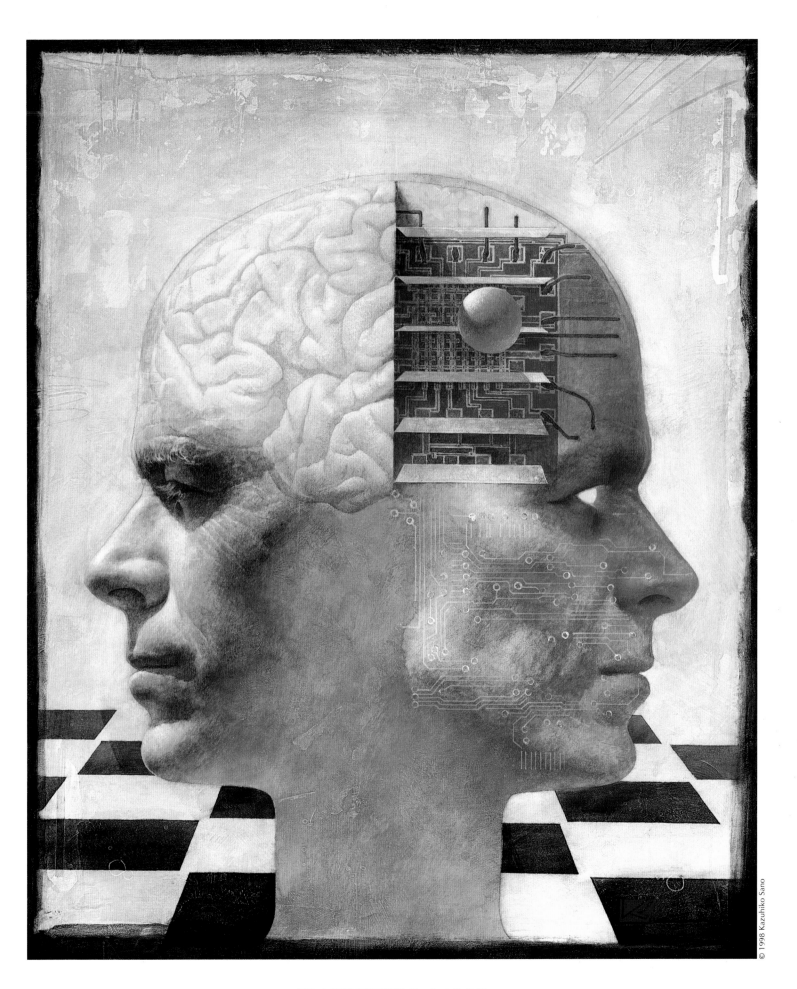

KAZUHIKO SANO

© 1998 Kazuhiko Sano

227

RENARD

REPRESENTS

VALERIE
SINCLAIR

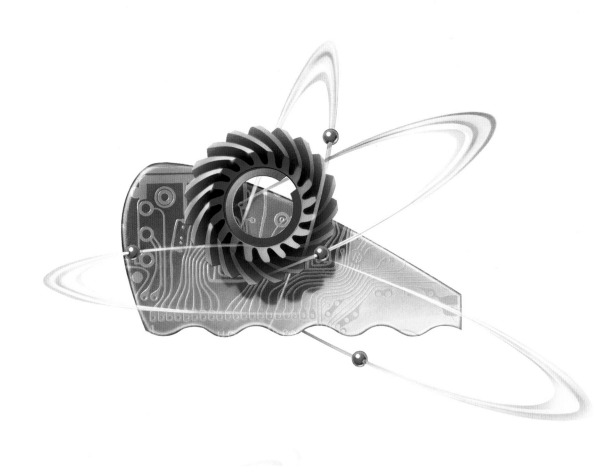

© 1998 Valerie Sinclair

RENARD REPRESENTS

■

TEL: 212•490•2450
FAX: 212•697•6828
www.renardrepresents.com

JUD
GUITTEAU

RENARD REPRESENTS

■

TEL: 212•490•2450
FAX: 212•697•6828
www.renardrepresents.com

© 1998 Jud Guitteau

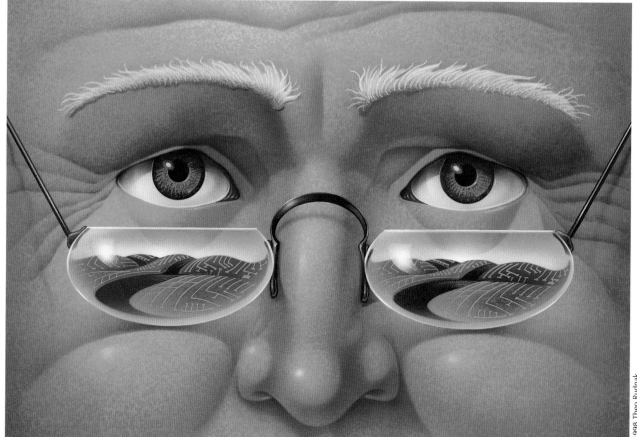

© 1998 Theo Rudnak

RENARD

REPRESENTS

BILL
CIGLIANO

RENARD REPRESENTS

■

TEL: 212•490•2450
FAX: 212•697•6828
www.renardrepresents.com

R E N A R D
REPRESENTS

GARY
ELDRIDGE

RENARD REPRESENTS

■

TEL: 212•490•2450
FAX: 212•697•6828
www.renardrepresents.com

RENARD
REPRESENTS

WENDY
GROSSMAN

© 1998 Wendy Grossman

RENARD REPRESENTS

■

TEL: 212•490•2450
FAX: 212•697•6828
www.renardrepresents.com

© 1998 Robert Rodriguez

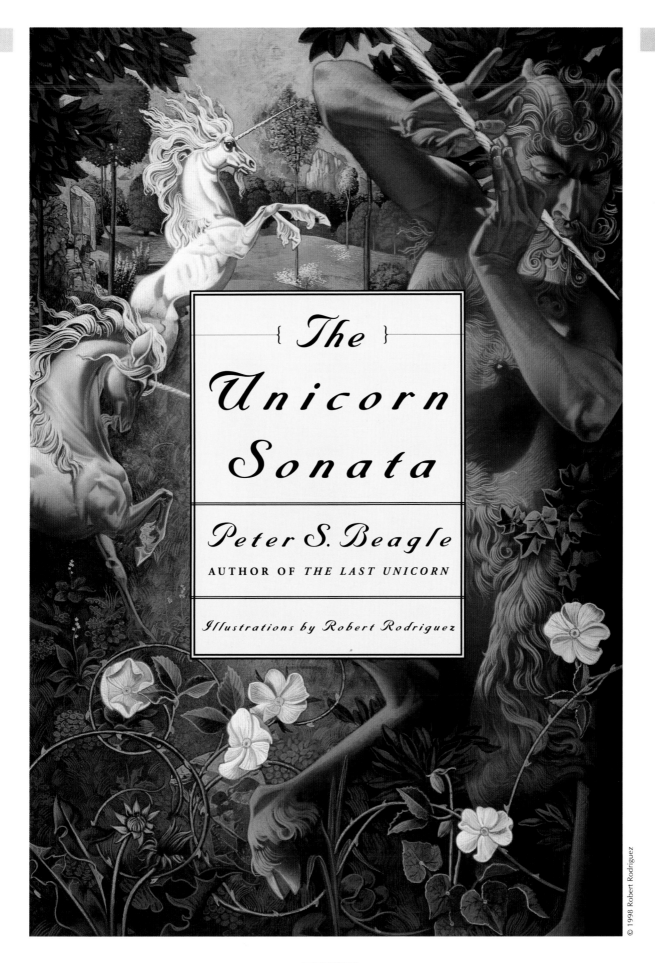

The Unicorn Sonata

Peter S. Beagle

AUTHOR OF *THE LAST UNICORN*

Illustrations by Robert Rodriguez

RODRIGUEZ

RENARD
REPRESENTS

MATSU

RENARD REPRESENTS

■

TEL: 212•490•2450
FAX: 212•697•6828
www.renardrepresents.com

243

RENARD

REPRESENTS

JONATHAN
HERBERT

STATE-OF-
THE-ART 3D
MODELING FOR
PRINT AND
ANIMATION
■
CALL FOR BOOK
OR REEL

RENARD
REPRESENTS

JEFFREY
PELO

RENARD REPRESENTS

■

Tel: 212•490•2450
Fax: 212•697•6828
www.renardrepresents.com

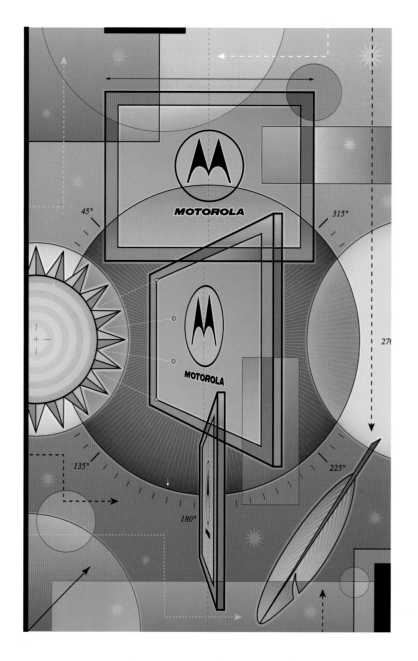

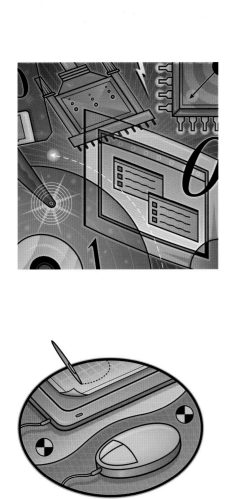

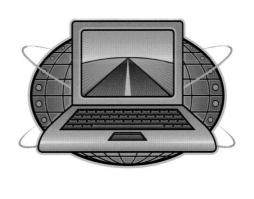

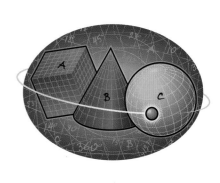

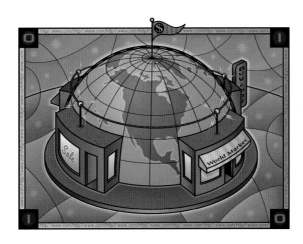

© 1998 Jeffrey Pelo

© 1998 John Martin

248

RENARD

REPRESENTS

ROGER HILL

RENARD REPRESENTS

■

Tel: 212•490•2450
Fax: 212•697•6828
www.renardrepresents.com

RENARD
REPRESENTS

STEVE
BJÖRKMAN

RENARD REPRESENTS

∎

TEL: 212•490•2450
FAX: 212•697•6828
www.renardrepresents.com

WAYNE McLOUGHLIN

© 1998 Wayne McLoughlin

RENARD

REPRESENTS

JOHN MacDONALD

Digitally
Enhanced
Scratchboard

RENARD

REPRESENTS

JULIE
MORRIS

RENARD REPRESENTS

■

TEL: 212•490•2450
FAX: 212•697•6828
www.renardrepresents.com

©1998 Julie Morris

RENARD
REPRESENTS

ROB
BROOKS

RENARD REPRESENTS

∎

Tel: 212•490•2450
Fax: 212•697•6828
www.renardrepresents.com

RENARD

REPRESENTS

RENÉ
MILOT

RENARD REPRESENTS

■

TEL: 212•490•2450
FAX: 212•697•6828
www.renardrepresents.com

© 1998 René Milot

STU
SUCHIT

© 1998 Stu Suchit

KIM
WHITESIDES

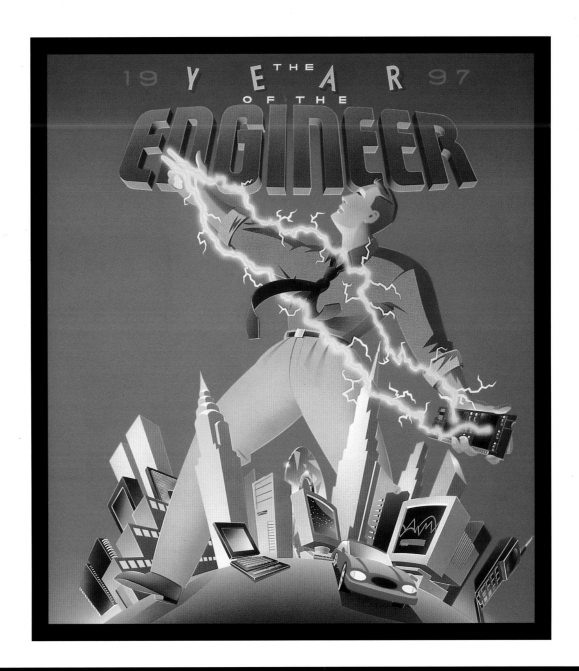

© 1998 Kim Whitesides

RENARD
REPRESENTS

RICHARD
NEWTON

© 1998 Richard Newton

RENARD

REPRESENTS

MICHAEL McGURL

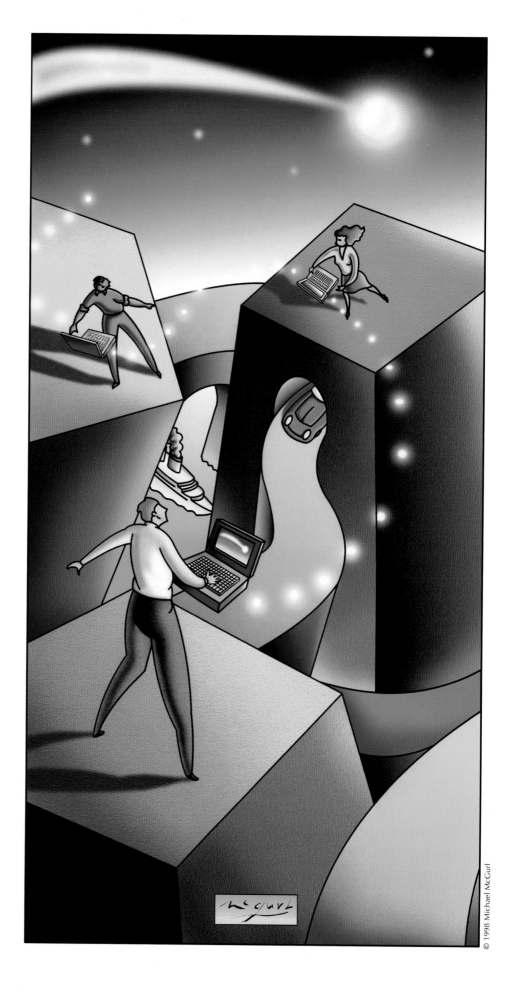

RENARD REPRESENTS

■

TEL: 212•490•2450
FAX: 212•697•6828
www.renardrepresents.com

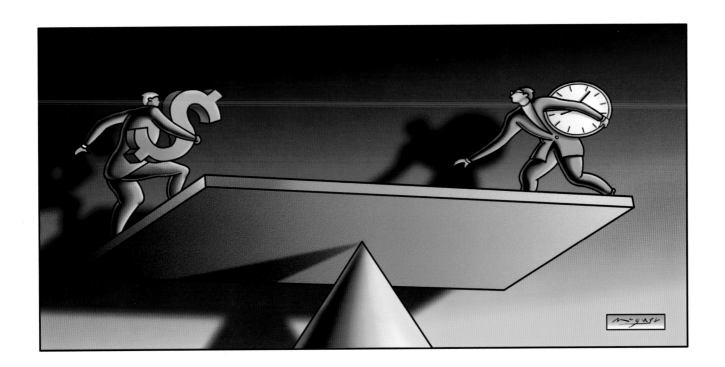

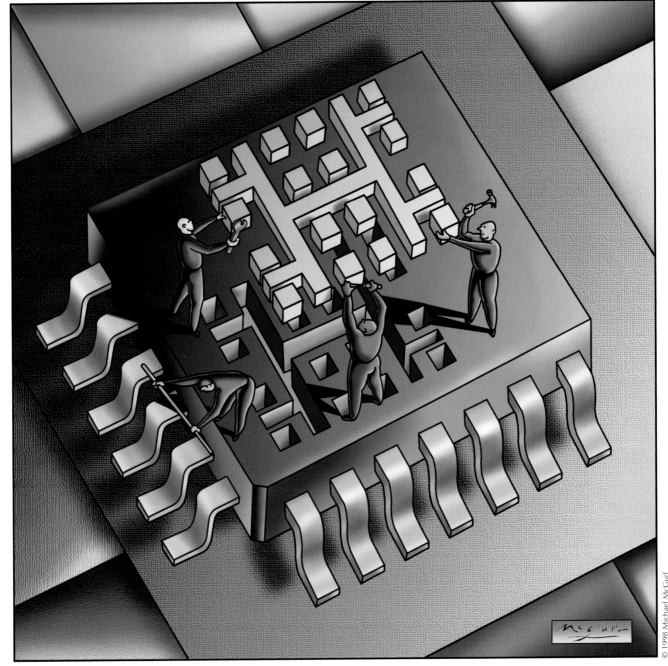

KEVIN POPE

© 1998 Kevin Pope

Everyday,... is a *cartoon* day.

El Hombre Loco

GOVERNORS STATE UNIVERSITY
UNIVERSITY PARK
IL 60466

STÉPHAN
DAIGLE

© 1998 Stéphan Daigle

© 1998 Stéphan Daigle

DAN
GARROW

© 1998 Dan Garrow

RENARD
REPRESENTS

JAMES
BOZZINI

RENARD REPRESENTS

■

TEL: 212•490•2450
FAX: 212•697•6828
www.renardrepresents.com

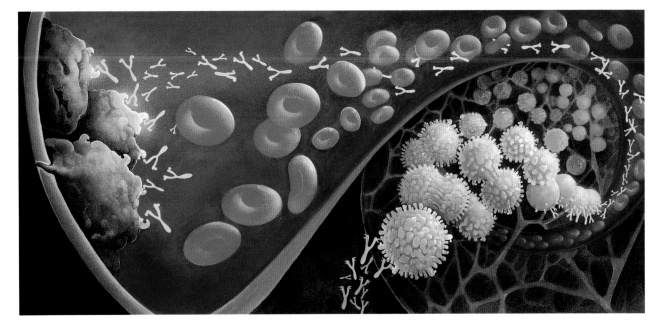

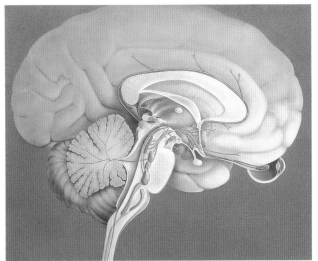

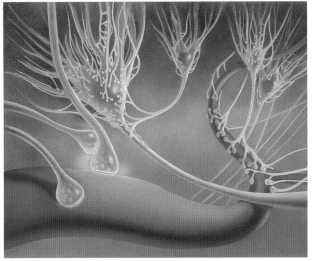

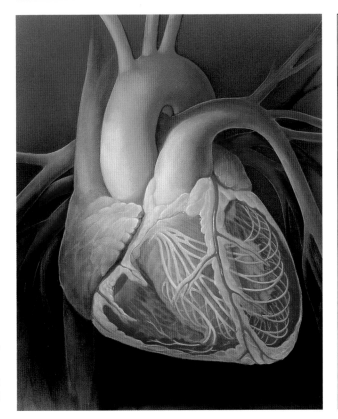

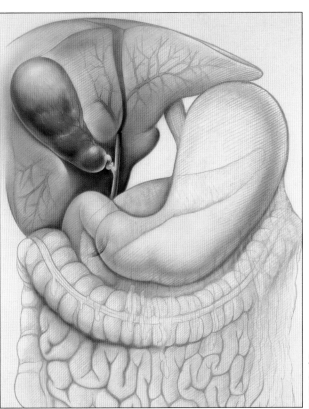

© 1998 Carol Donner

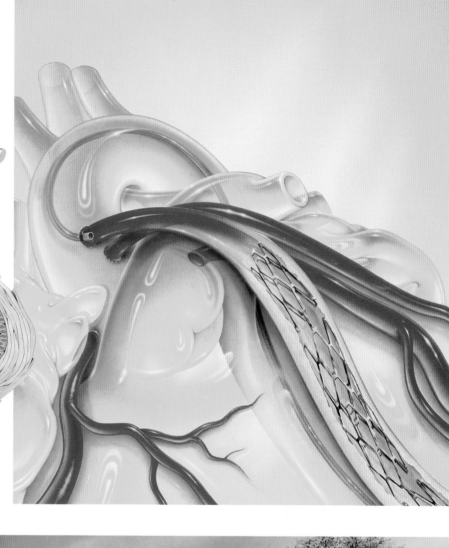

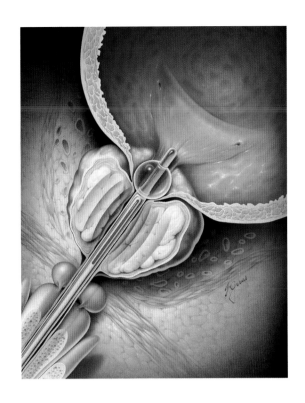

loudvik akopyan

(S)

(S)hann

(S)harron

john berg

(S)

DRAGON'S FLIGHT

竜

(S)

peter bollinger

(S)hannon

peter bollinger

digital illustration and animation

(S)

(S)hannon

Shannon Associates L.L.C. 327 east 89th street ■ suite 3E ■ new york ■ new york ■ 10128
phone 212 831 5650 ■ facsimile 212 831 6241
1306 alabama street ■ huntington beach ■ california ■ 92648
phone 714 969 7766 ■ facsimile 714 374 3744

steve brodner

illustration and animation

(S)

(S)

greg call

(S)hannon

Shannon Associates L.L.C.   327 east 89th street ■ suite 3E ■ new york ■ new york ■ 10128
phone 212 831 5650 ■ facsimile 212 831 6241
1306 alabama street ■ huntington beach ■ california ■ 92648
phone 714 969 7766 ■ facsimile 714 374 3744

THELMA HOUSTON • CECE PENISTON • PHOEBE SNOW • LOIS WALDEN • ALBERTINA WALKER

THE SISTERS OF GLORY

GOOD NEWS IN HARD TIMES

jim carroll

(S)

Shannon Associates L.L.C.   327 east 89th street ■ suite 3E ■ new york ■ new york ■ 10128

(S)

richard cowdrey

(S\hannon

mike dietz

(S)hannon

Shannon Associates L.L.C.   327 east 89th street ▪ suite 3E ▪ new york ▪ new york ▪ 10128
phone 212 831 5650 ▪ facsimile 212 831 6241
1306 alabama street ▪ huntington beach ▪ california ▪ 92648
phone 714 969 7766 ▪ facsimile 714 374 3744

NONE OF THIS IS REAL — Lao Tzu

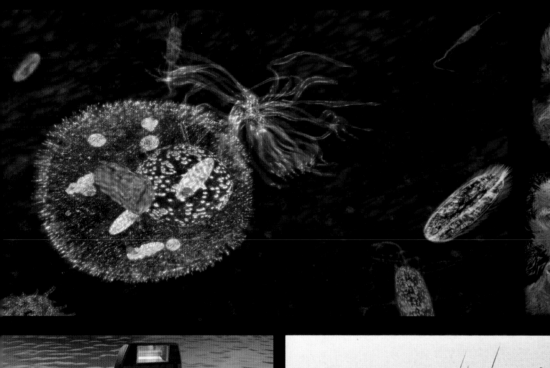

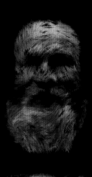

Design By Eastman Kodak Co.

toby welles/design core

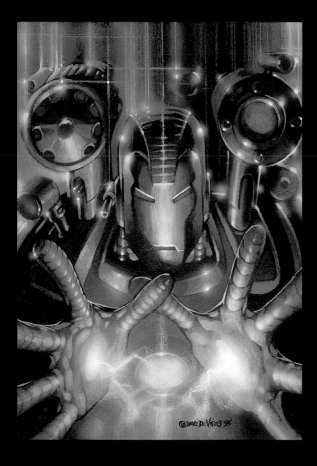

dave devries

mark elliott

(S)

Shannon Associates L.L.C.   327 east 89th street ■ suite 3E ■ new york ■ new york ■ 10128
phone 212 831 5650 ■ facsimile 212 831 6241
1306 alabama street ■ huntington beach ■ california ■ 92648
phone 714 969 7766 ■ facsimile 714 374 3744

tristan elwell

(S)hannon

Shannon Associates L.L.C.   327 east 89th street ■ suite 3E ■ new york ■ new york ■ 10128

phone 212 831 5650 ■ facsimile 212 831 6241

1306 alabama street ■ huntington beach ■ california ■ 92648

(S)

patrick faricy

(S)hannon

Shannon Associates L.L.C.   327 east 89th street ■ suite 3E ■ new york ■ new york ■ 10128
phone 212 831 5650 ■ facsimile 212 831 6241
1306 alabama street ■ huntington beach ■ california ■ 92648
phone 714 969 7766 ■ facsimile 714 374 3744

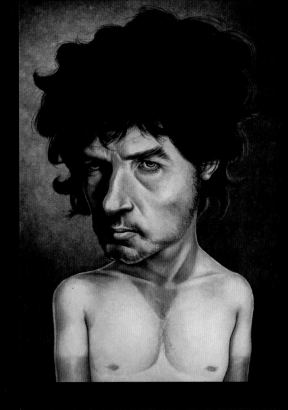

THE POSIES
AMAZING DISGRACE

IT'S 'INDEPENDENCE DAY' MEETS 'PULP FICTION'!
SEE IT ALL...IN 'BLACK'!

MEN IN BLACK

TEN WEEKS
OF SHOOTING!
A YEAR IN POST-
PRODUCTION!
$80 MILLION
WORTH
OF ALIENS!
BIG-ASS GUNS!
AND EYE-POPPING
EFFECTS!

STARRING WILL SMITH / TOMMY LEE JONES

(S)

tim gabor

Nº1 FOO FIGHTERS

FOO FIGHTERS

DEBUT ALBUM OUT NOW!

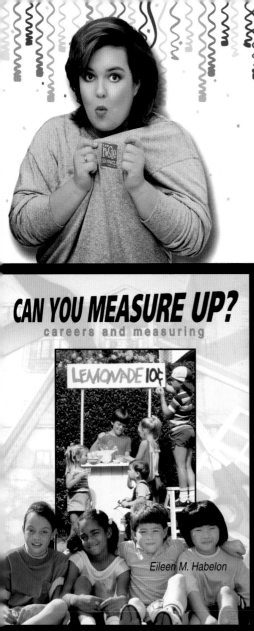

CAN YOU MEASURE UP?

careers and measuring

LEMONADE 10¢

Eileen M. Habelon

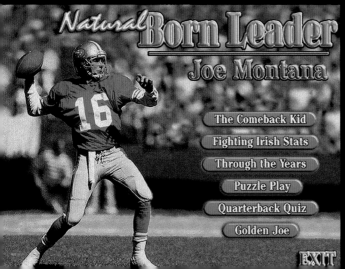

Natural *Born Leader*

Joe Montana

16

The Comeback Kid

Fighting Irish Stats

Through the Years

Puzzle Play

Quarterback Quiz

Golden Joe

EXIT

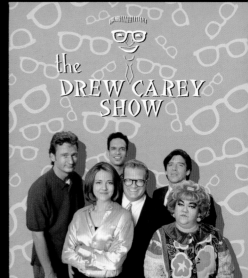

the
DREW CAREY
SHOW

MANHATTAN
SOHO

Metropolitan Transportation Authority
Arts for Transit

Artist Stephen Johnson's striking light and shadow study of an industrial fire escape evokes both Soho's manufacturing heritage and the urban beauty of this famous artistic community.

MTA New York City Transit

Subway
Prince St
Spring St
Spring St

Broadway-Lafayette
Houston St

Bus
M1* M5 M10 M21

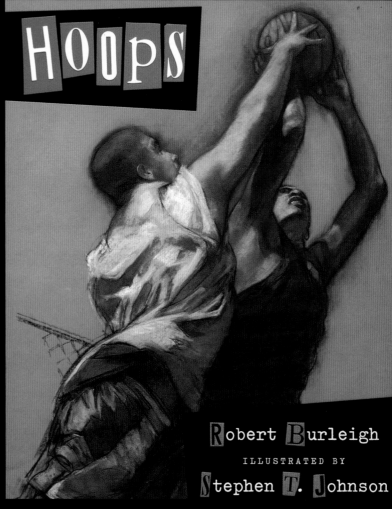

HOOPS

Robert Burleigh

ILLUSTRATED BY

Stephen T. Johnson

SAMUEL ADAMS
WINTER CLASSICS

THE BOSTON BEER CO.

6 Distinctive Beer Styles
2 BOTTLES EACH OF HONEY PORTER, CRANBERRY LAMBIC,
OLD FEZZIWIG ALE, WINTER LAGER, BOSTON LAGER, SCOTCH ALE

stephen t. johnson

(S)

(S)hanno

Women of Wonder

THE CLASSIC YEARS

Science Fiction by Women from the 1940s to the 1970s

Edited and with an introduction and notes by **PAMELA SARGENT**

A Harvest Original

michael köelsch

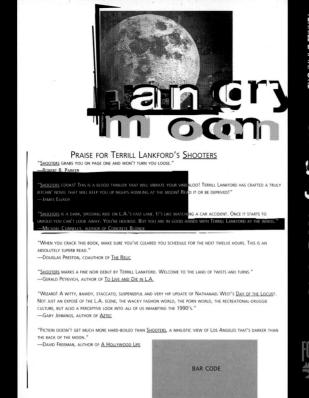

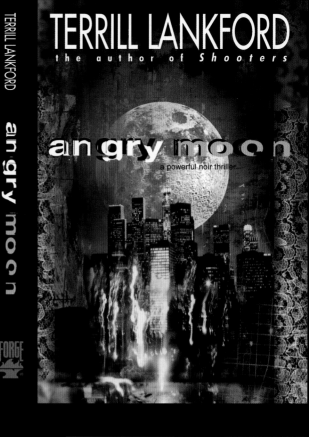

PRAISE FOR TERRILL LANKFORD'S SHOOTERS

"SHOOTERS grabs you on page one and won't turn you loose."
—ROBERT B. PARKER

"SHOOTERS cooks! This is a blood thriller that will vibrate your vindaloo! Terrill Lankford has crafted a truly bitchin' novel that will keep you up nights howling at the moon! Read it or be deprived!"
—JAMES ELLROY

"SHOOTERS is a dark, speeding ride on L.A.'s fast lane. It's like watching a car accident. Once it starts to unfold you can't look away. You're hooked. But you are in good hands with Terrill Lankford at the wheel."
—MICHAEL CONNELLY, author of CONCRETE BLONDE

"When you crack this book, make sure you've cleared you schedule for the next twelve hours. This is an absolutely superb read."
—DOUGLAS PRESTON, coauthor of THE RELIC

"SHOOTERS marks a fine noir debut by Terrill Lankford. Welcome to the land of twists and turns."
—GERALD PETIEVICH, author of TO LIVE AND DIE IN L.A.

"WIZARD! A witty, bawdy, staccato, suspenseful and very hip update of Nathanael West's DAY OF THE LOCUST. Not just an exposé of the L.A. scene, the wacky fashion world, the porn world, the recreational-druggie culture, but also a perceptive look into ALL of us inhabiting the 1990's."
—GARY JENNINGS, author of AZTEC

"Fiction doesn't get much more hard-boiled than SHOOTERS, a nihilistic view of Los Angeles that's darker than the back of the moon."
—DAVID FREEMAN, author of A HOLLYWOOD LIFE

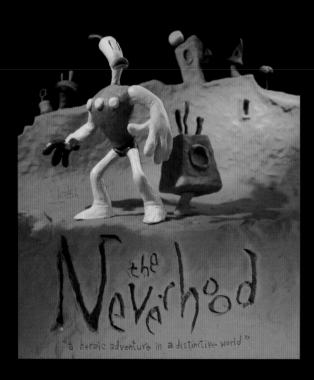

michael köelsch
design & digital illustration

The Black Cat

Edgar A. Poe

(S)hannon

dave kramer

(S)

cliff nielsen

(S)hannon

Shannon Associates L.L.C.   327 east 89th street ■ suite 3E ■ new york ■ new york ■ 10128
phone 212 831 5650 ■ facsimile 212 831 6241
1306 alabama street ■ huntington beach ■ california ■ 92648
phone 714 969 7766 ■ facsimile 714 374 3744

(S)

carlos torres

TORRES

(S)hannon

Shannon Associates L.L.C.   327 east 89th street ■ suite 3E ■ new york ■ new york ■ 10128

JACQUELINE DEDELL

REPRESENTING

Scott	BALDWIN
Cathie	BLECK
Edward	BRIANT
Alicia	BUELOW
Brian	CAIRNS
Ron	CHAN
Ivan	CHERMAYEFF
Nancy	DAVIS
Dolores	FAIRMAN
David	FRAMPTON
Linda	FRICHTEL
Gene	GREIF
Hayes	HENDERSON
Bryan	LEISTER
Griesbach	MARTUCCI
Frank	MILLER
Max	MILLER
Paula	MUNCK
Merle	NACHT
Edward	PARKER
Kimberly	BULCKEN ROOT
Fletcher	SIBTHORP
Linda	DeVITO SOLTIS
Gordon	STUDER
Richard	TUSCHMAN
Mick	WIGGINS
Heidi	YOUNGER
Chermayeff	& GEISMAR, INC.

JACQUELINE DEDELL INC., ARTIST REPRESENTATIVE

58 WEST 15TH STREET, NEW YORK, NEW YORK, 10011 **TEL:** (212) 741-2539 **FAX:** (212) 741-4660

WEBSITE: www.showcase.com

IBM

WINSTAR

Mick WIGGINS

JACQUELINE DeDELL _Inc_ 58 WEST 15TH STREET, NEW YORK, NY, 10011 **TEL:** (212) 741-2539 **FAX:** (212) 741-4660
WEBSITE: www.showcase.com

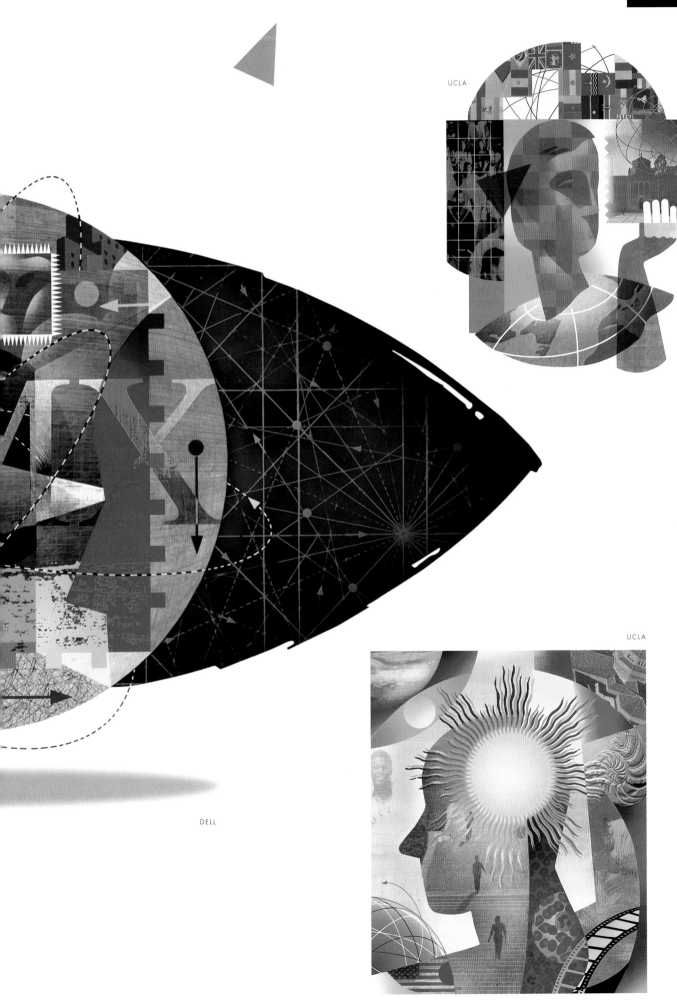

UCLA

UCLA

DELL

JACQUELINE DEDELL Inc

Cathie BLECK

JACQUELINE DEDELL Inc 58 WEST 15TH STREET, NEW YORK, NY 10011 TEL: (212) 741-2539 FAX: (212) 741-4660 WEBSITE: www.showcase.com

HABITAT FOR HUMANITY INTERNATIONAL

THE WASHINGTON POST

JACQUELINE DEDELL

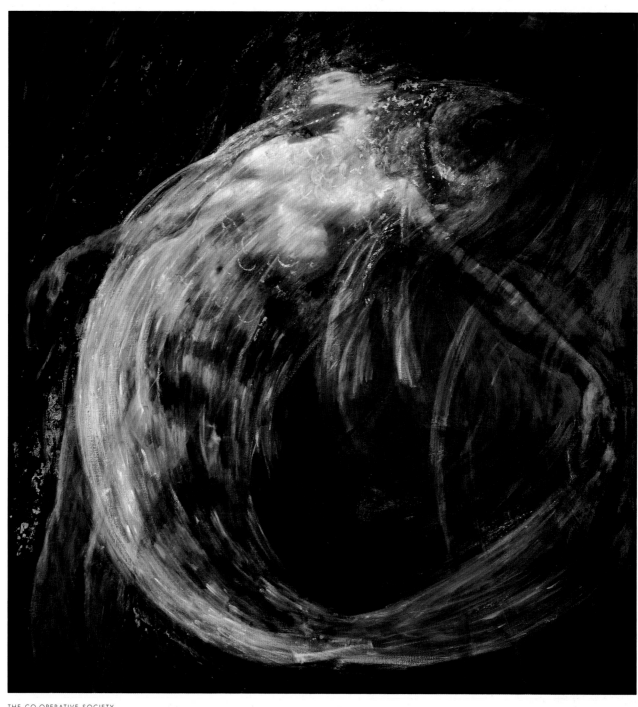

THE CO-OPERATIVE SOCIETY

Fletcher SIBTHORP

RANDOM CENTURY PUBLISHING

BOOKS ETC.

JACQUELINE DELL

Inc

Ron CHAN

JACQUELINE DEDELL Inc 58 WEST 15TH STREET, NEW YORK, NY, 10011 **TEL:** (212) 741-2539 **FAX:** (212) 741-4660
WEBSITE: www.showcase.com

REPRESENTING *Ron* CHAN

THE JOHN F. KENNEDY CENTER FOR THE PERFORMING ARTS

JACQUELINE DeDELL *Inc*

HEINEY & CRAIG / ELECTROGLAS ANNUAL REPORT

Richard TUSCHMAN

JACQUELINE DEDELL Inc. 58 WEST 15TH STREET, NEW YORK, NY, 10011 **TEL:** (212) 741-2539 **FAX:** (212) 741-4660
WEBSITE: www.showcase.com

KIPLINGER'S

CAPERS CLEVELAND DESIGN / COMNET '97

JACQUELINE DEDELL Inc

GOURMET MAGAZINE

THE HARTFORD COURANT

Merle NACHT

JACQUELINE DEDELL Inc. 58 WEST 15TH STREET, NEW YORK, NY, 10011 **TEL:** (212) 741-2539 **FAX:** (212) 741-4660
WEBSITE: www.showcase.com

NISSAN JAPAN / DYNA SEARCH

NISSAN JAPAN / DYNA SEARCH

FAMILY FUN MAGAZINE

TENNIS MAGAZINE

JACQUELINE DEDELL *Inc.*

341

CLARKE THOMPSON / NEW YORK TIMES MEDIA KIT

MONACO VIOLA

BOOK OF THE MONTH CLUB

MONACO VIOLA

CHILD MAGAZINE

Linda FRICHTEL

CATHOLIC HEALTH ASSOCIATION

Gordon STUDER

MACWORLD

Gordon STUDER

JACQUELINE DEDELL Inc 58 WEST 15TH STREET, NEW YORK, NY, 10011 **TEL:** (212) 741-2539 **FAX:** (212) 741-4660
WEBSITE: www.showcase.com

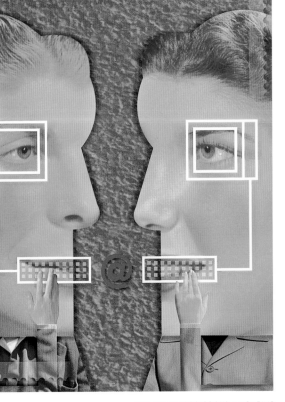

CIO COMMUNICATIONS

SAN FRANCISCO FOCUS MAGAZINE

MEN'S HEALTH

JACQUELINE DEDELL

Inc

THE NEW YORKER

BUSINESS WEEK

Ed BRIANT

JACQUELINE DEDELL Inc 58 WEST 15TH STREET, NEW YORK, NY, 10011 **TEL:** (212) 741-2539 **FAX:** (212) 741-4660
WEBSITE: www.showcase.com

THE NEW YORK TIMES

HBO

HBO

SKY MAGAZINE / PACE COMMUNICATIONS

THE GREENWICH WORKSHOP

WINDJAMMER DAYS

Ed PARKER

EAST DESIGN

THE WASHINGTON POST

Nancy DAVIS

JACQUELINE DeDELL Inc 58 WEST 15TH STREET, NEW YORK, NY, 10011 **TEL:** (212) 741-2539 **FAX:** (212) 741-4660
WEBSITE: www.showcase.com

HANNA ANDERSSON

HANNA ANDERSSON

JACQUELINE DeDELL Inc

VISA

Frank MILLER

VISA

PIONEER / DAY MEDIA & COMMUNICATIONS

HOUSE & HOME MAGAZINE

Paula MUNCK

JACQUELINE DEDELL Inc. 58 WEST 15TH STREET, NEW YORK, NY, 10011   TEL: (212) 741-2539 FAX: (212) 741-4660
WEBSITE: www.showcase.com

JACQUELINE DEDELL Inc.

355

through these veins
I can see everything
a compass of gold and steel grey
oceans and crows
dark loud secrets
the conflict of sky and sea
through these veins
you can see everything
a room of fire and rain
sirens and swells
fear and desire
silent questions for all I see
through these veins
I can see everything
a compass of gold and steel grey
oceans and crows
dark loud secrets

Alicia BUELOW

JACQUELINE DeDELL Inc. 58 WEST 15TH STREET, NEW YORK, NY, 10011 TEL: (212) 741-2539 FAX: (212) 741-4660 WEBSITE: www.showcase.com

Look

ADOBE SYSTEMS INCORPORATED

JACQUELINE DeDELL
Inc.
a compass of gold and grey

AUDUBON MAGAZINE

INFOWORLD

INFOWORLD

SMART MONEY

HARCOURT BRACE

JACQUELINE DEDELL *Inc*

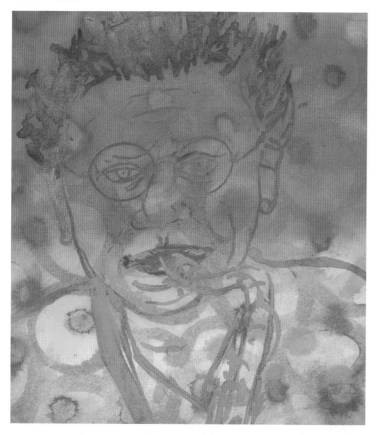

Max MILLER

JACQUELINE DeDELL Inc

PIMCO ADVISORS

Scott BALDWIN

SMG DESIGN

OPPENHEIMER FUNDS

7000

6500

6000

PIMCO ADVISORS

JACQUELINE DeDELL Inc

BOZELL PALMER BONNER – CANADA

EARL GEE DESIGN / SYMANTEC CORP

GRID / 2 INTERNATIONAL / MANHATTAN BAGEL

Heidi YOUNGER

HADASSAH

To view more work, see Graphic Artists Guild Directory of Illustration Vol. 8-14.

GEORGE ANGELINI

DORON BEN-AMI

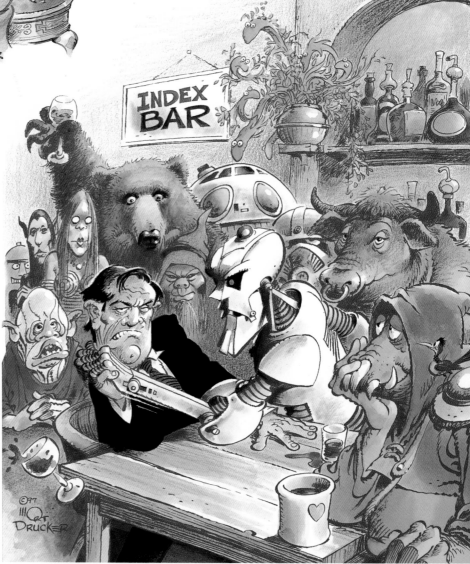

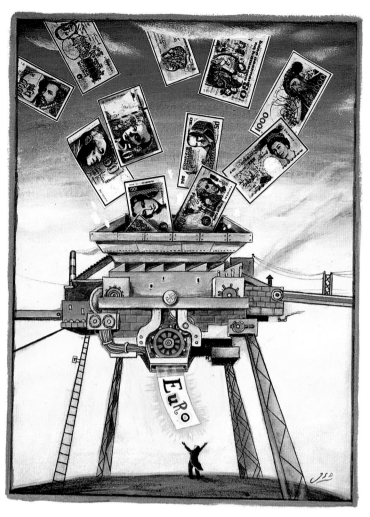

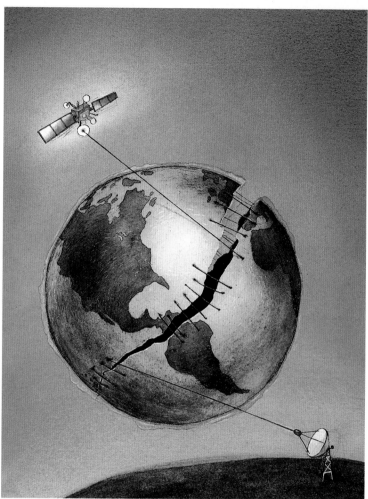

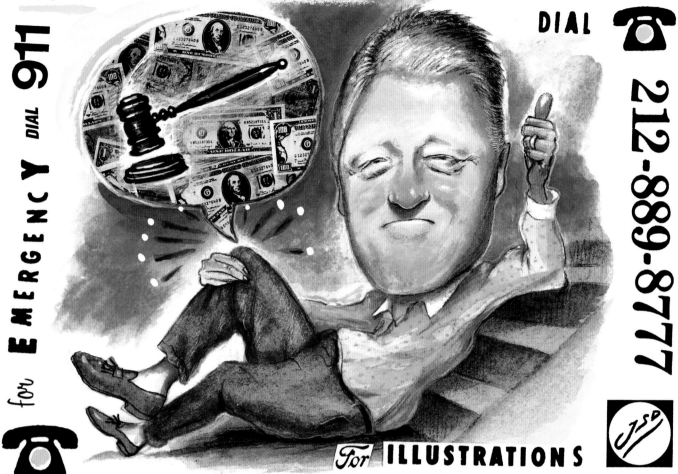

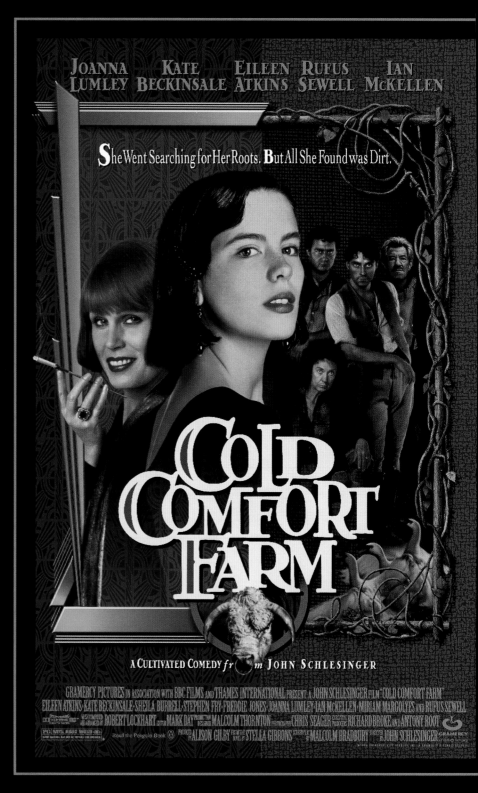

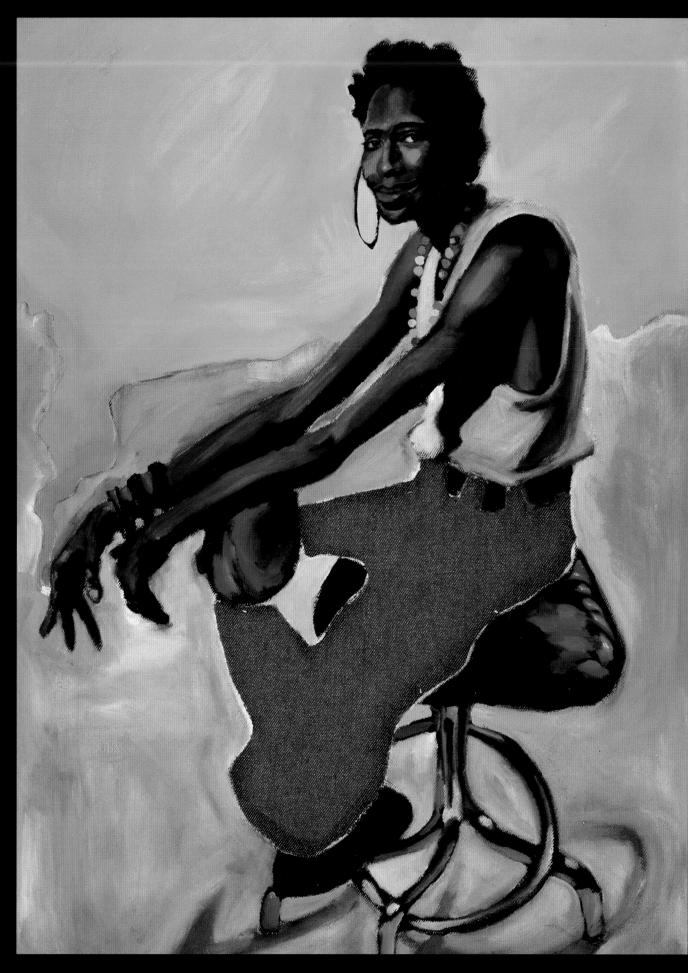

 GAIL THURM & SARI LEVY in New York City (212) 889-8777 / fax (212) 447-1475 / e-mail: artconyc@ix.netcom.com

 GAIL THURM & SARI LEVY in New York City (212) 889-8777 / fax (212) 447-1475 / e-mail: artconyc@ix.netcom.com
JEFF PALMER outside New York City (203) 222-8777 / fax (203) 454-9940 / e-mail: artcoct@snet.net

RAY DOWNING
STUDIO MACBETH INC.
3D COMPUTER GRAPHICS
FOR PRINT AND VIDEO

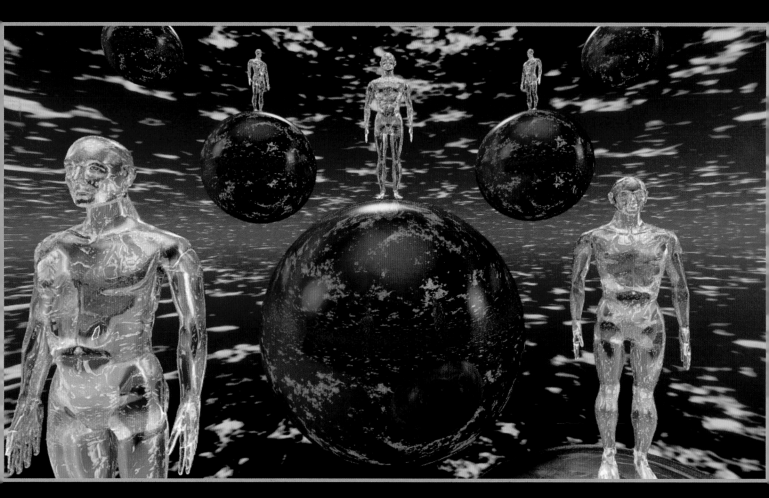

RAY DOWNING
STUDIO MACBETH INC.
3D COMPUTER GRAPHICS
FOR PRINT AND VIDEO

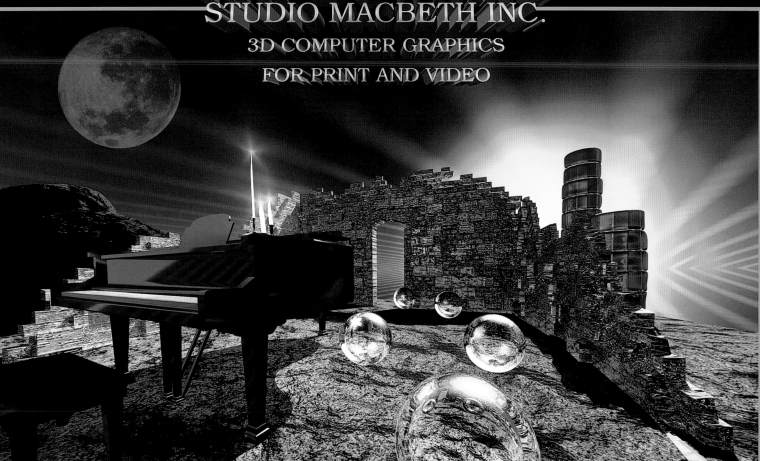

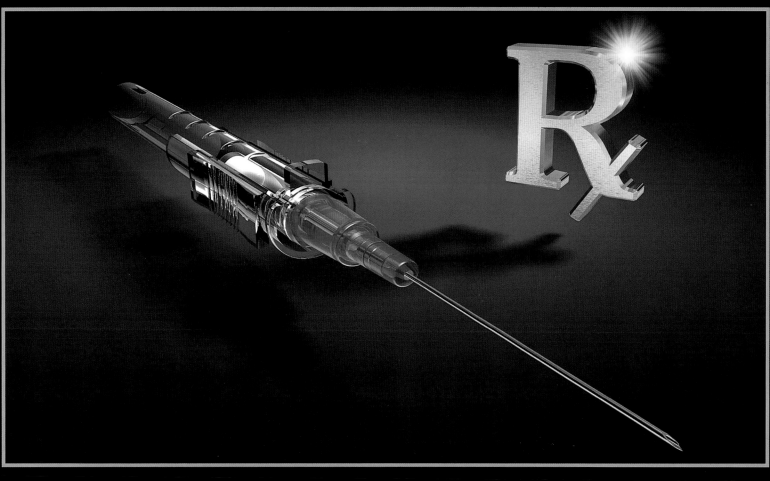

Rudolph Giuliani and the Big Apple

Woman in Red

Madeline Albright

GAIL THURM & SARI LEVY in New York City (212) 889-8777 / fax (212) 447-1475 / e-mail: artconyc@ix.netcom.com

JEFF PALMER outside New York City (203) 222-8777 / fax (203) 454-9940 / e-mail: artcoct@snet.net

Hackers Honeymoon

TM & © St.Pierre/Chlystek

TM & © Marvel Entertainment

TM & © Marvel Entertainment

GAIL THURM & SARI LEVY in New York City (212) 889-8777 / fax (212) 447-1475 / e-mail: artconyc@ix.netcom.com
JEFF PALMER outside New York City (203) 222-8777 / fax (203) 454-9940 / e-mail: artcoct@snet.net

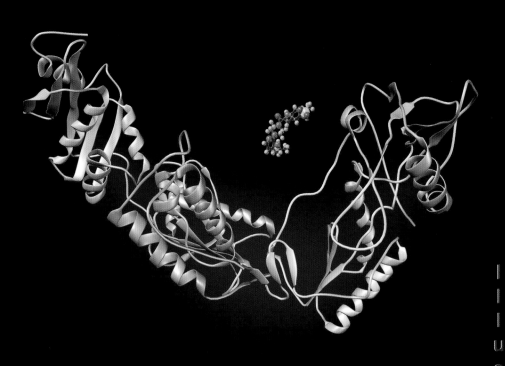

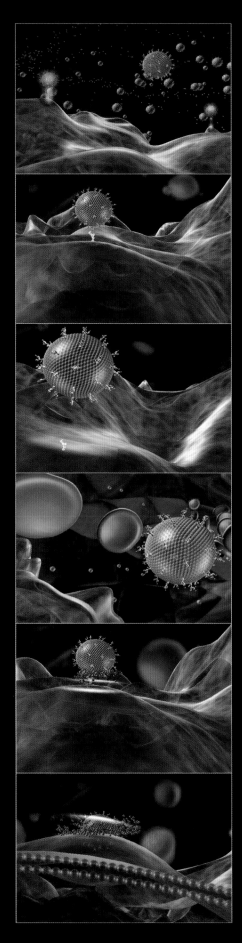

Illustration

Animation

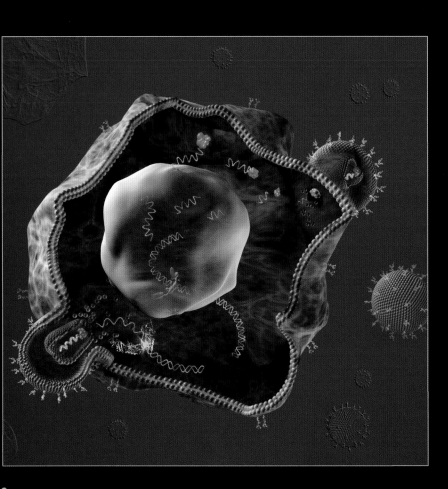

Illustration   Animation

GAIL THURM & SARI LEVY in New York City (212) 889-8777 / fax (212) 447-1475 / e-mail: artconyc@ix.netcom.com

ARTCO

GAIL THURM & SARI LEVY in New York City (212) 889-8777 / fax (212) 447-1475 / e-mail: artconyc@ix.netcom.com
JEFF PALMER outside New York City (203) 222-8777 / fax (203) 454-9940 / e-mail: artcoct@snet.net

The legendary Cadmus brought the alphabet and writing to the ancient Greeks and lives in eternity transformed as a snake.

wake up and go to work

J.T. MORROW
THE ART OF IMITATION

LINDA CANE

JENNY CAMPBELL

ANTHONY CERICOLA
MACINTOSH ILLUSTRATION

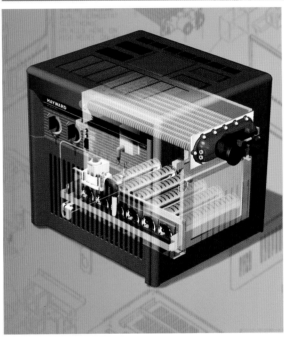

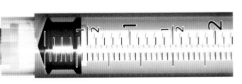

DEBORAH
WOLFE
LIMITED

731 N 24TH ST   PHILA PA 19130   www.deborahwolfeltd.com   215.232.6666   FAX 232.6585

ANDY MYER

DEBORAH
WOLFE
LIMITED

731 N 24TH ST   PHILA PA 19130   www.deborahwolfeltd.com   215.232.6666   FAX 232.6585

JONATHAN & GEORGINA ROSENBAUM
MACINTOSH ILLUSTRATION

STEVEN NAU

JOSEPH PAGE KOVACH

STEPHEN BAUER

DEBORAH
WOLFE
LIMITED

731 N 24TH ST   PHILA PA 19130   www.deborahwolfeltd.com   215.232.6666   FAX 232.6585

NICK ROTONDO

MACINTOSH ILLUSTRATION

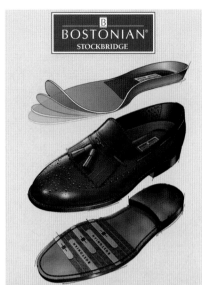

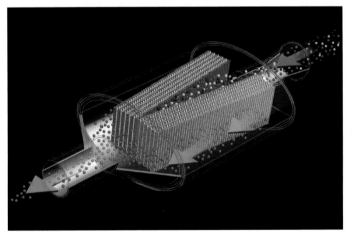

RICHARD WALDREP

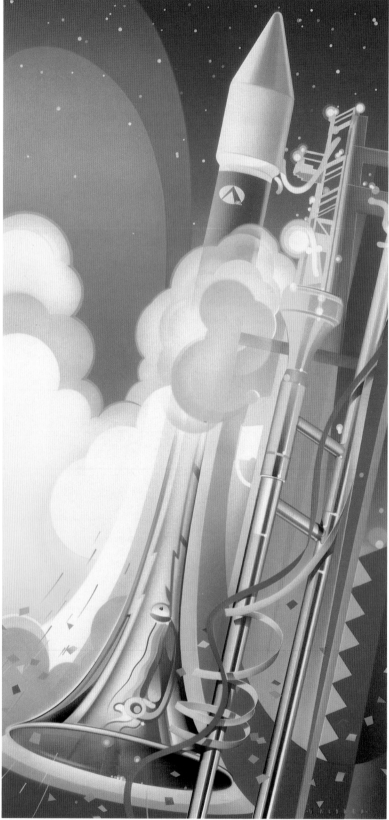

AMY WUMMER

DEBORAH
WOLFE
LIMITED

731 N 24TH ST   PHILA PA 19130   www.deborahwolfeltd.com   215.232.6666   FAX 232.6585

PATRICK GNAN

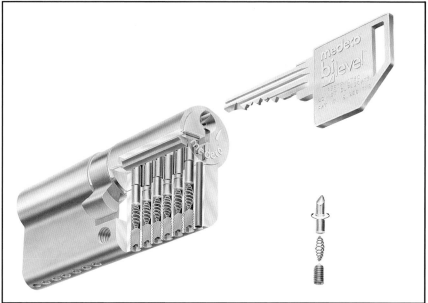

LISA POMERANTZ

DEBORAH
WOLFE
LIMITED

731 N 24TH ST   PHILA PA 19130   www.deborahwolfeltd.com   215.232.6666   FAX 232.6585

RANDY HAMBLIN

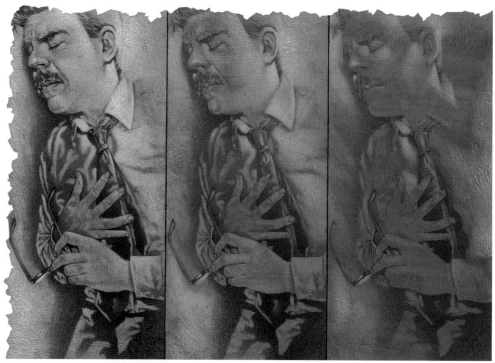

MARIANNE HUGHES

SKIP BAKER
MACINTOSH ILLUSTRATION

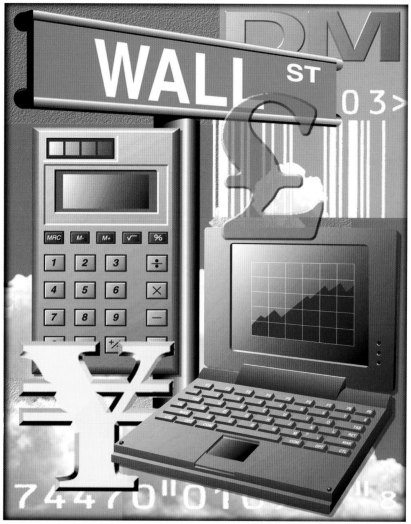

DEBORAH
WOLFE
LIMITED

731 N 24TH ST   PHILA PA 19130   www.deborahwolfeltd.com   215.232.6666   FAX 232.6585

LARRY WINBORG

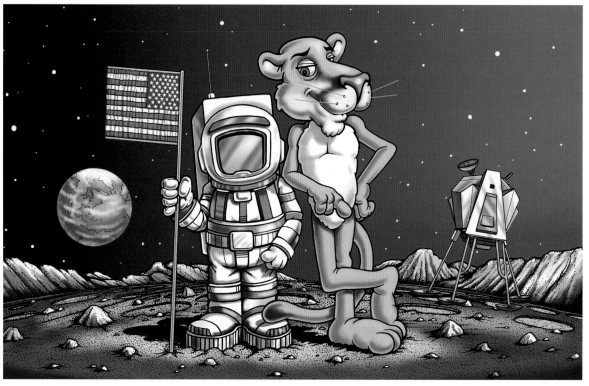

IRENA ROMAN

DEBORAH
WOLFE
LIMITED

731 N 24TH ST   PHILA PA 19130   www.deborahwolfeltd.com   215.232.6666   FAX 232.6585

JEFF FITZ-MAURICE

DEBORAH
WOLFE
LIMITED

731 N 24TH ST   PHILA PA 19130   www.deborahwolfeltd.com   215.232.6666   FAX 232.6585

LEIF PENG
MACINTOSH ILLUSTRATION

DEBORAH
WOLFE
LIMITED

731 N 24TH ST   PHILA PA 19130   www.deborahwolfeltd.com   215.232.6666   FAX 232.6585

SAUL ROSENBAUM

MACINTOSH ILLUSTRATION

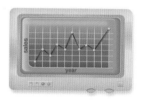

JOHN HOLM

Website: http://www.spar.org/americanart

Website: http://www.spar.org/americanart

ELAINE KURIE

Digital Illustration

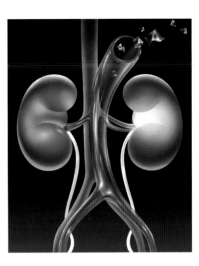

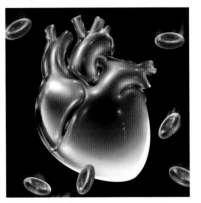

Kurie

LATER...

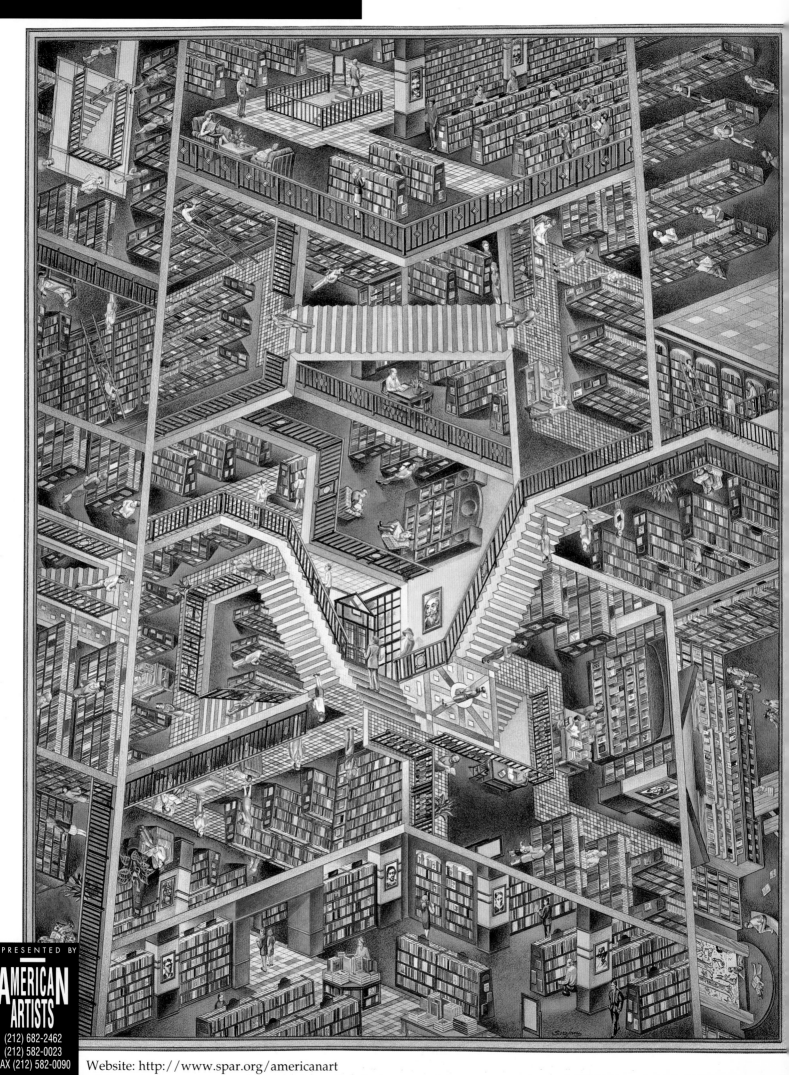

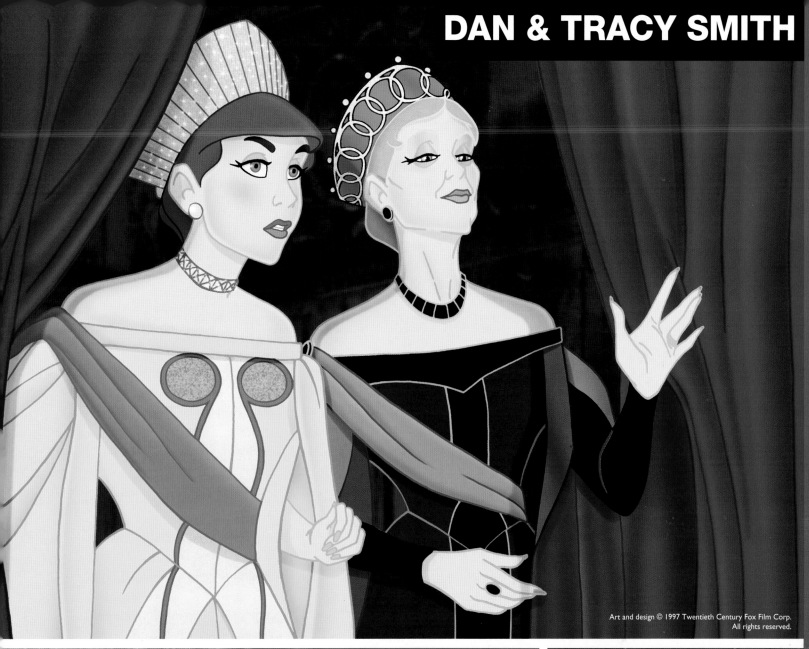

http://www.spar.org

ABSOLUT KOSOLAPOV

REPRESENTED BY

AMERICAN ARTISTS

(212) 682-2462
(212) 582-0023
FAX (212) 582-0090

REPRESENTED BY

AMERICAN ARTISTS

(212) 682-2462
(212) 582-0023
FAX (212) 582-0090

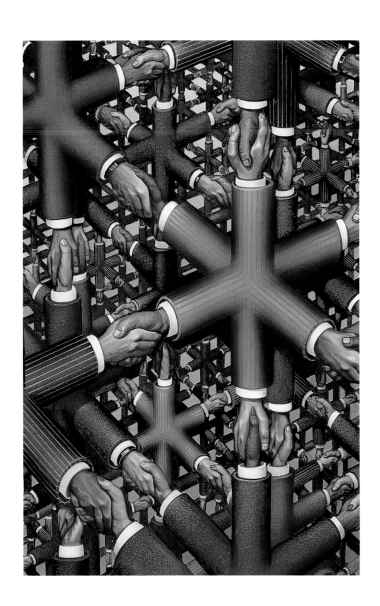

TONY RANDAZZO

TONY RANDAZZO

JERRY LOFARO

REPRESENTED BY

AMERICAN ARTISTS

(212) 682-2462
(212) 582-0023
FAX (212) 582-0090

Website: http://www.spar.org/americanart

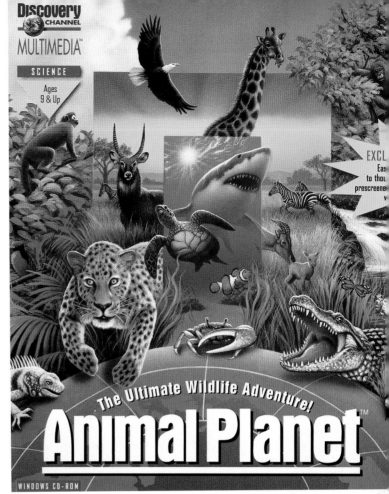

MIKE JAROSZKO

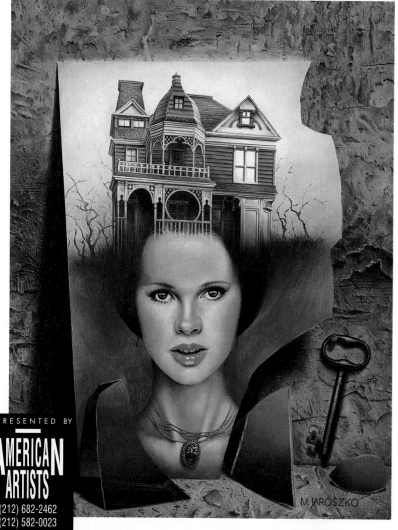

Website: http://www.spar.org/americanart

Website: http://www.spar.org/americanart

GARTH GLAZIER

PRESENTED BY
AMERICAN ARTISTS
(212) 682-2462
(212) 582-0023
X (212) 582-0090

Website: http://www.spar.org/americanart

KENT GAMBLE

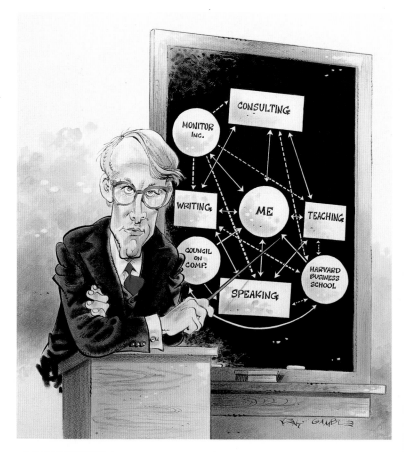

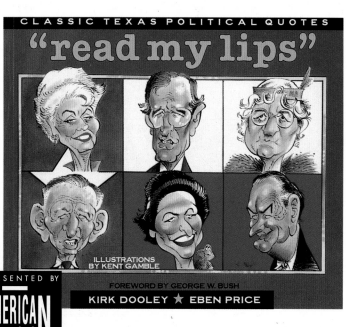

STUDIO
805 374 9634
818 880 1524

JOHN and PHILLIP HOM

FAX
805 374 9647
818 880 1525

SHAWN McKELVEY

 Cary & Company Ph:(404)296-9666/Fx:(404)296-1537

McKelvey Studio: (562)432-8122

Website: http://www.spar.org/americanart

JONATHAN WRIGHT

"RUHN" RANSLEY KENIN

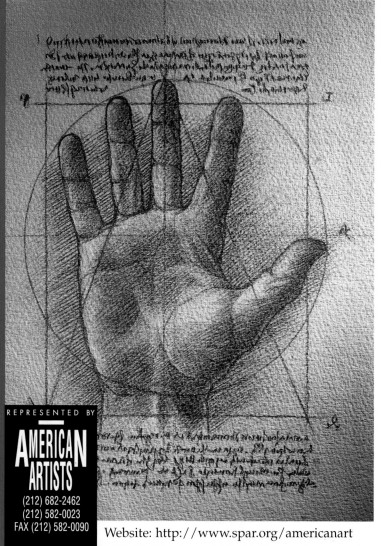

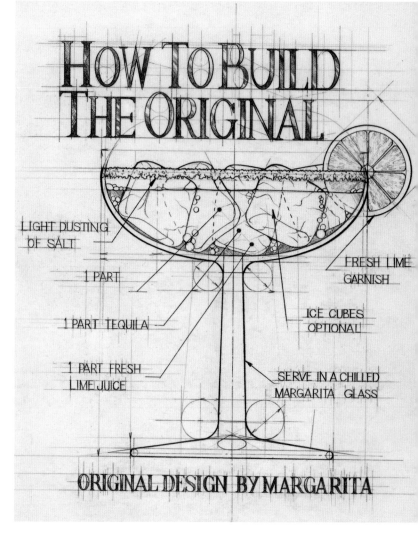

LIGHT DUSTING
OF SALT

1 PART

1 PART TEQUILA

1 PART FRESH
LIME JUICE

FRESH LIME
GARNISH

ICE CUBES
OPTIONAL!

SERVE IN A CHILLED
MARGARITA GLASS

ORIGINAL DESIGN BY MARGARITA

Website: http://www.spar.org/americanart

KIMBLE

David Kimble
915 • 729 • 4802

CKI MORGA
VICKI MORGAN & GAIL GAYNIN
VICKI
MORGAN
ASSOCIATES
194 THIRD AVE
NYC 10003
PH:(212)475-0440 FX:(212)353-8538

VICKI MORGAN & GAIL GAYNIN
VICKI MORGAN ASSOCIATES
194 THIRD AVE
NYC 10003
PH:(212)475-0440 FX:(212)353-8538

LAURIE LAFRANCE

VICKI MORGAN & GAIL GAYNIN

VICKI
MORGAN
ASSOCIATES

194 THIRD AVE
NYC 10003

PH:(212)475-0440 FX:(212)353-8538

Darci Kistler, New York City Ballet, in *Swan Lake*. Photo reference: Paul Kolnik

JOANIE SCHWARZ

j. schwarz

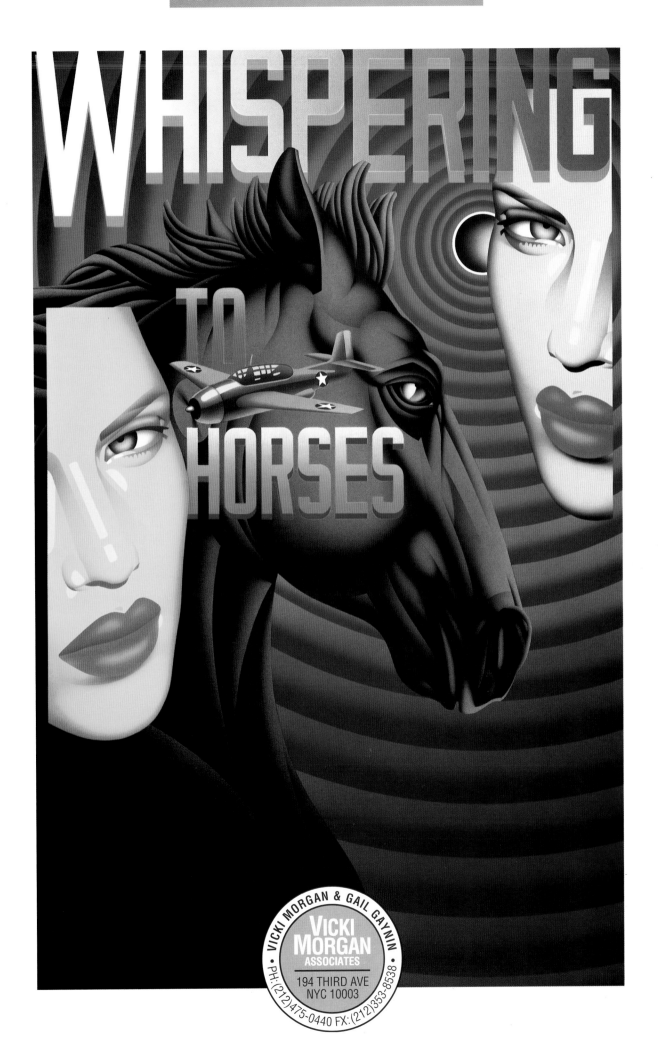

VICKI MORGAN & GAIL GAYNIN

VICKI
MORGAN
ASSOCIATES

194 THIRD AVE
NYC 10003

PH:(212)475-0440 FX:(212)353-8538

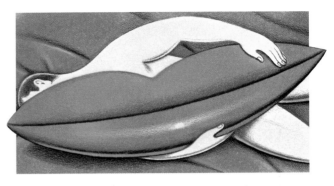

BEPPE GIACOBBE

ELIZABETH ROSEN

man did not weave this web of life He is merely a strand of it — whatever he does to the web he does to himself. - chief seartle

VICKI MORGAN & GAIL GAYNIN
VICKI MORGAN
ASSOCIATES
194 THIRD AVE
NYC 10003
PH: (212) 475-0440 FX: (212) 353-8538

STEAM

VICKI MORGAN & GAIL GAYNIN

VICKI
MORGAN
ASSOCIATES
194 THIRD AVE
NYC 10003
PH:(212)475-0440 FX:(212)353-8538

Gervasio Gallardo

LAVATY

(212) 427-5632

L

FRANK & JEFF LAVATY
(212) 427-5632 Fax: (212) 427-6372
Associates:
Kevin Cassidy & Ebba Lavaty

Representing
J O H N   B E R K E Y

L FRANK & JEFF LAVATY

(212) 427-5632 Fax: (212) 427-6372
Associates:
Kevin Cassidy & Ebba Lavaty

Representing
CHRIS DUKE

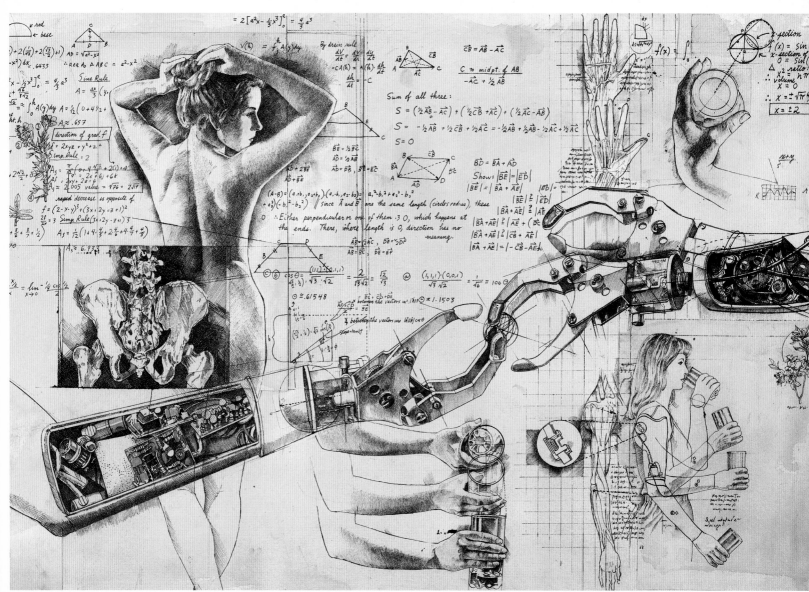

L

FRANK & JEFF LAVATY
(212) 427-5632 Fax: (212) 427-6372
Associates:
Kevin Cassidy & Ebba Lavaty

Representing

CHRIS DUKE

L
FRANK & JEFF LAVATY
(212) 427-5632 Fax: (212) 427-6372
Associates:
Kevin Cassidy & Ebba Lavaty

Representing
BEN VERKAAIK

L

FRANK & JEFF LAVATY
(212) 427-5632 Fax: (212) 427-6372
Associates:
Kevin Cassidy & Ebba Lavaty

Representing
BEN VERKAAIK

483

L

fRANK & Jeff LAVATY
(212) 427-5632 Fax: (212) 427-6372
Associates:
Kevin Cassidy & Ebba Lavaty

Representing
TIM HILDEBRAND

fRANK & JEff LAVATY
(212) 427-5632 Fax: (212) 427-6372
Associates:
Kevin Cassidy & Ebba Lavaty

Representing
D O N   D E M E R S

L

fRANK & JEff LAVATY
(212) 427-5632 Fax: (212) 427-6372
Associates:
Kevin Cassidy & Ebba Lavaty

Representing
L O R I   A N Z A L O N E

L

fRANK & JEff LAVATY
(212) 427-5632 Fax: (212) 427-6372
Associates:
Kevin Cassidy & Ebba Lavaty

Representing
L O R I A N Z A L O N E

FRANK & JEFF LAVATY

(212) 427-5632 Fax: (212) 427-6372
Associates:
Kevin Cassidy & Ebba Lavaty

Representing
PETER SCANLAN

FRANK & JEFF LAVATY
(212) 427-5632 Fax: (212) 427-6372
Associates:
Kevin Cassidy & Ebba Lavaty

Representing
PETER SCANLAN

L

FRANK & JEFF LAVATY
(212) 427-5632 Fax: (212) 427-6372
Associates:
Kevin Cassidy & Ebba Lavaty

Representing
CARLOS
OCHAGAVIA

L

FRANK & JEFF LAVATY
(212) 427-5632 Fax: (212) 427-6372
Associates:
Kevin Cassidy & Ebba Lavaty

Representing

D O M E N I C K
D ' A N D R E A

L

FRANK & JEFF LAVATY
(212) 427-5632 Fax: (212) 427-6372
Associates:
Kevin Cassidy & Ebba Lavaty

Representing
CRAIG ATTEBERY

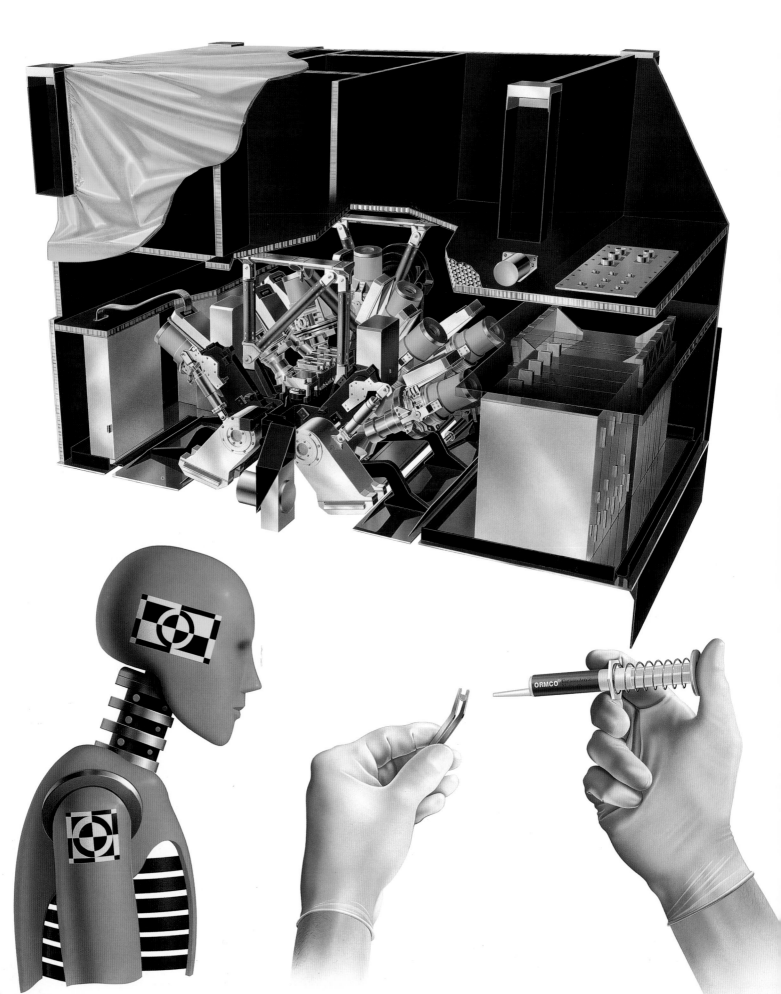

L

FRANK & JEFF LAVATY
(212) 427-5632 Fax: (212) 427-6372
Associates:
Kevin Cassidy & Ebba Lavaty

Representing
CRAIG ATTEBERY

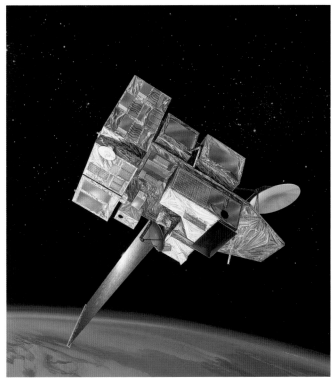

fRANK & JEfF LAVATY
(212) 427-5632 Fax: (212) 427-6372
Associates:
Kevin Cassidy & Ebba Lavaty

Representing
JOHN PAUL GENZO

L

FRANK & JEFF LAVATY
(212) 427-5632 Fax: (212) 427-6372
Associates:
Kevin Cassidy & Ebba Lavaty

Representing
ROBERT LOGRIPP

L

FRANK & JEFF LAVATY
(212) 427-5632 Fax: (212) 427-6372
Associates:
Kevin Cassidy & Ebba Lavaty

Representing
D E E   D E L O Y

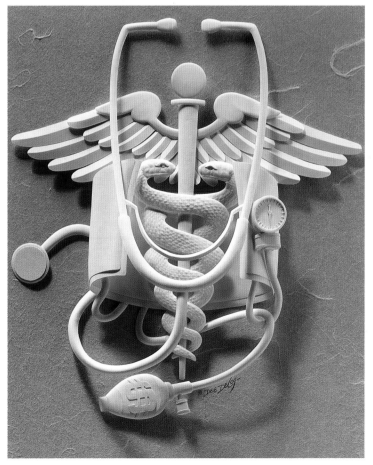

Peter Siu

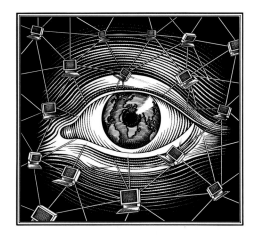

 **ph 212 627-1554 · fax 212 627-1719**
contact Betty Krichman or Ron Puhalski • 89 Fifth Avenue Suite 901, New York, NY 10003

Art works   **Peter Fiore**
              2 1 2   6 2 7 - 1 5 5 4

Peter Fiore

 **ph 212 627-1554 · fax 212 627-1719**
contact Betty Krichman or Ron Puhalski • 89 Fifth Avenue Suite 901, New York, NY 10003

Ellis Chappell

Paul Bachem

Artworks **ph 212 627-1554 • fax 212 627-1719**
contact Betty Krichman or Ron Puhalski • 89 Fifth Avenue Suite 901, New York, NY 10003

Molly O'Gorman

 **Art**works   **ph 212 627-1554 • fax 212 627-1719**
contact Betty Krichman or Ron Puhalski • 89 Fifth Avenue Suite 901, New York, NY 10003

Dan Brown

Matthew Rotunda

 **ph 212 627-1554 · fax 212 627-1719**
contact Betty Krichman or Ron Puhalski • 89 Fifth Avenue Suite 901, New York, NY 10003

Patrick D. Milbourn

 Art works

ph 212 627-1554 • fax 212 627-1719
contact Betty Krichman or Ron Puhalski • 89 Fifth Avenue Suite 901, New York, NY 10003

Mike Harper

 Art works
ph 212 627-1554 · fax 212 627-1719
contact Betty Krichman or Ron Puhalski • 89 Fifth Avenue Suite 901, New York, NY 10003

Dennis Lyall

Artworks **ph 212 627-1554 · fax 212 627-1719**
contact Betty Krichman or Ron Puhalski • 89 Fifth Avenue Suite 901, New York, NY 10003

 **Art**works **ph 212 627-1554 · fax 212 627-1719**
contact Betty Krichman or Ron Puhalski · 89 Fifth Avenue Suite 901, New York, NY 10003

Bob Dombrowski

Artworks **ph 212 627-1554 · fax 212 627-1719**
contact Betty Krichman or Ron Puhalski • 89 Fifth Avenue Suite 901, New York, NY 10003

Tony Meers

 **Art**works **ph 212 627-1554 · fax 212 627-1719**
contact Betty Krichman or Ron Puhalski • 89 Fifth Avenue Suite 901, New York, NY 10003

512

Adrian Chesterman

Artworks

ph 212 627-1554 · fax 212 627-1719
contact Betty Krichman or Ron Puhalski • 89 Fifth Avenue Suite 901, New York, NY 10003

Harry Burman

 **Art**works — **ph 212 627-1554 • fax 212 627-1719**
contact Betty Krichman or Ron Puhalski • 89 Fifth Avenue Suite 901, New York, NY 10003

Rick Lovell

Stephen Gardner

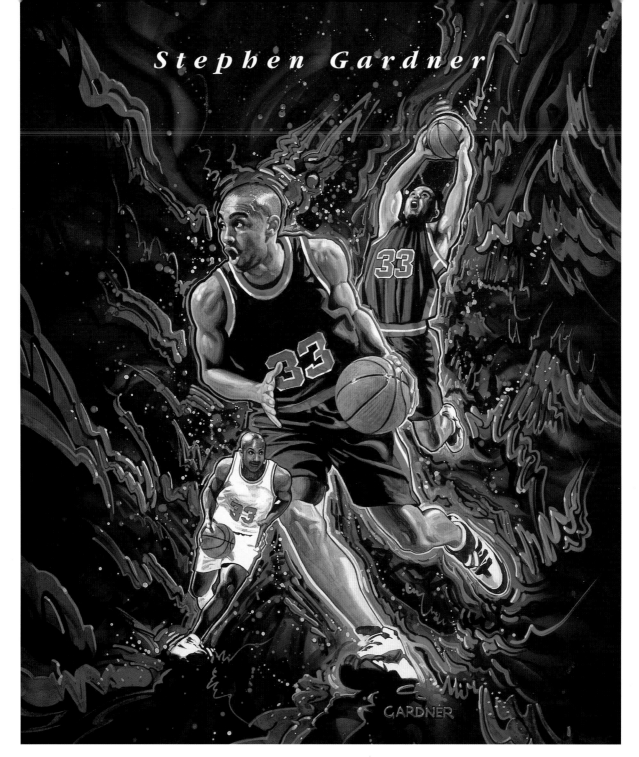

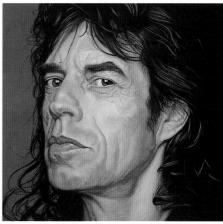

FRANCO ACCORNERO

BRIAN CALLANAN

DENISE CRAWFORD

MANUEL GEERINCK

FRED HILLIARD

MIKE HODGES

LINGTA KUNG

BERTRAND LEPAUTREMAT

FRED LYNCH

MICHELE MANNING

DAVID O'KEEFE

RIK OLSON

PIERRE-PAUL PARISEAU

MICHAEL PLANK

MARY THELEN

leff

Jerry Leff Associates

(212) 697-8525

Fax (212) 949-1843

www.theispot.com/rep/jleff

e-mail: JLAssoc@worldnet.att.net

LE NOUVEL OBSERVATEUR

AMERICAN EXPRESS MAGAZINE

LE MONDE

FRED LYNCH

VIKING PENGUIN

NEW ENGLAND BUSINESS MAGAZINE

CIO MAGAZINE

BERTRAND

LE PAUTREMAT

CONQUEROR

INVESTIR

S.I.A.A.P.

OLIO

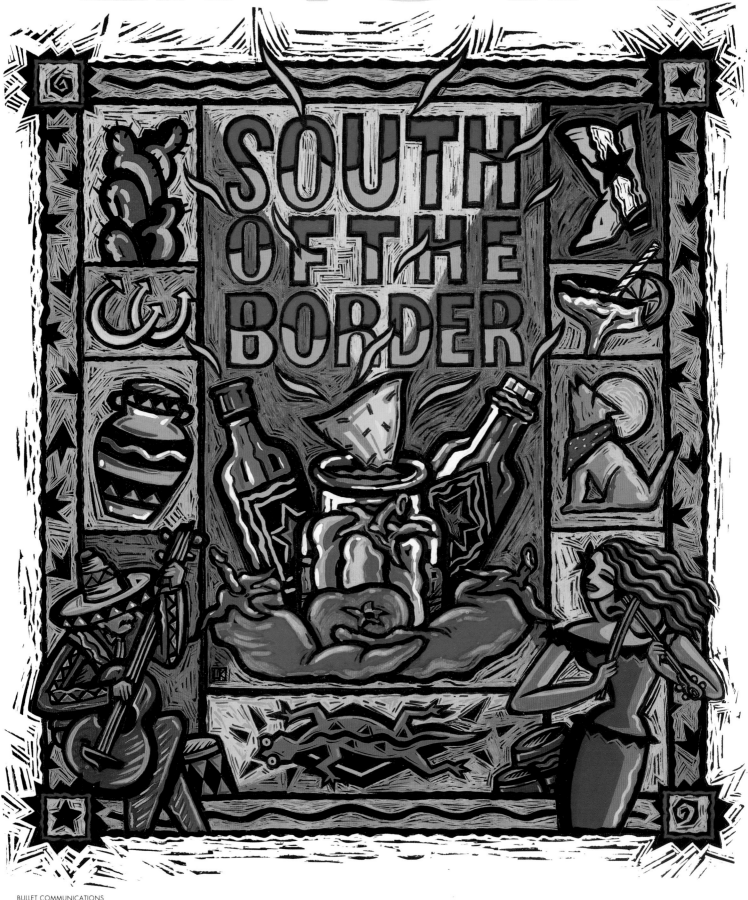

BULLET COMMUNICATIONS

(212) 697-8525
www.theispot.com/rep/jleff

JerrY leff
ASSOCIATES

Fax (212) 949-1843
e-mail: JLAssoc@worldnet.att.net

MICHAEL
PLANK

RIK
OLSON

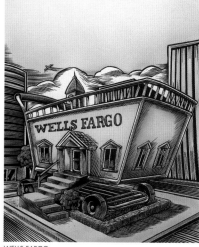

WELLS FARGO

CHEVRON

DFS, LTD.

WELLS FARGO

524

FIDELITY INVESTMENTS

CONSECO, INC. 1996 ANNUAL REPORT

"Are we to take it the outlook is upbeat?"

"This isn't a dream, Ed. It's reality!"

CONSECO, INC. 1996 ANNUAL REPORT

(212) 697-8525
www.theispot.com/rep/jleff

Jerry Leff ASSOCIATES

Fax (212) 949-1843
e-mail: JLAssoc@worldnet.att.net

DAVID
O'KEEFE

DOW JONES INVESTMENT ADVISOR

MIKE
HODGES

SARASOTA MAGAZINE

MBL & WESTERN LIFE

VIRGINIA COMMONWEALTH UNIVERSITY

INFUSION MAGAZINE

WORLD MARKETING ALLIANCE

PIERRE-PAUL
P A R I S E A U

TELESAT

NEW YEAR'S CARD

COMPUTER WORLD JOURNAL

HEALTHCARE FORUM JOURNAL

PIERRE-PAUL

P A R I S E A U

WADSWORTH PUBLISHING

MICHELE
M A N N I N G

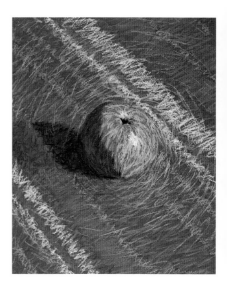

ALLYN & BACON

SIMON & SCHUSTER

(212) 697-8525
www.theispot.com/rep/jleff

Jerry Jeff
ASSOCIATES

Fax **(212) 949-1843**
e-mail: JLAssoc@worldnet.att.net

West
Jan Collier
(415) 383-9026
Fax **(415) 383-9037**

DENISE
CRAWFORD

(212) 697-8525
www.theispot.com/rep/jleff

Jerry Leff
ASSOCIATES

Fax **(212) 949-1843**
e-mail: JLAssoc@worldnet.att.net

THE HELEN

MARY

Enchantment in the Woods

MARY

Around the World

PRENTICE HALL

FITCH

FITCH

FITCH

BRIAN
C A L L A N A N

ANDERSEN CONSULTING

FRANCO
A C C O R N E R O

FRANCO
A C O R N E R O

John Manders

Leonid Gore

REPRESENTED BY

Harriet Kasak

TELEPHONE 212•675•5719
FACSIMILE 212•675•6341
E•MAIL HKPfolio@aol.com
http://www.spar.org

Kathi Ember

Mike Reed

Nan Brooks

REPRESENTED IN
CALIFORNIA BY

Rosenthal Represents

TELEPHONE 818•222•5445
FACSIMILE 818•222•5650

REPRESENTED IN
NEW YORK BY

Harriet Kasak

TELEPHONE 212•675•5719
FACSIMILE 212•675•6341
E•MAIL HKPfolio@aol.com
http://www.spar.org

REPRESENTED IN
CHICAGO BY

Holly Hahn

TELEPHONE 312•338•7110
FACSIMILE 312•338•7004

Abby Carter

REPRESENTED BY

Harriet Kasak

TELEPHONE 212•675•5719
FACSIMILE 212•675•6341
E•MAIL HKPfolio@aol.com
http://www.spar.org

George Ulrich

Paul Meisel

REPRESENTED BY

Harriet Kasak

TELEPHONE 212•675•5719
FACSIMILE 212•675•6341
E•MAIL HKPfolio@aol.com
http://www.spar.org

545

Anne Kennedy

REPRESENTED BY

Harriet Kasak

TELEPHONE 212•675•5719
FACSIMILE 212•675•6341
E•MAIL HKPfolio@aol.com
http://www.spar.org

Randy Verougstraete

REPRESENTED BY

Harriet Kasak

TELEPHONE 212•675•5719
FACSIMILE 212•675•6341
E•MAIL HKPfolio@aol.com
http://www.spar.org

Eldon Doty

Stephanie O'Shaughnessy

REPRESENTED BY

Harriet Kasak

TELEPHONE 212•675•5719
FACSIMILE 212•675•6341
E•MAIL HKPfolio@aol.com
http://www.spar.org

Renée Daily

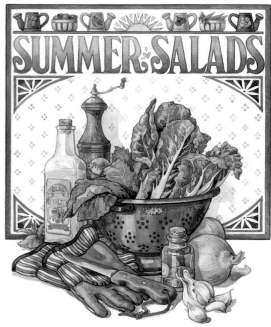

REPRESENTED IN
CALIFORNIA BY

Rosenthal Represents

TELEPHONE 818•222•5445
FACSIMILE 818•222•5650

REPRESENTED IN
NEW YORK BY

Harriet Kasak

TELEPHONE 212•675•5719
FACSIMILE 212•675•6341
E•MAIL HKPfolio@aol.com
http://www.spar.org

REPRESENTED IN
PHILADELPHIA BY

Carol Francisco

TELEPHONE 610•667•2378
FACSIMILE 610•667•4308

Rémy Simard

REPRESENTED BY

Harriet Kasak

TELEPHONE 212•675•5719
FACSIMILE 212•675•6341
E•MAIL HKPfolio@aol.com
http://www.spar.org

SOPHIE ALLPORT   CHRISTIAN BIRMINGHAM   IZHAR COHE

455 W 23RD

MATTHEW COOK   PENNY DANN   ANDREW DAVIDSON   GRAHA

NUMBER 8D

EVERNDEN   JODY HEWGILL   CHARLOTTE KNOX   JOH

& SALLY HEFLIN
THE ARTWORKS

LAWRENCE PETER MALONE   DESDEMONA McCANNO

NY NY 10011

SARAH McMENEMY   ANTON MORRIS   ANNIKA NELSO

TELEPHONE

HANOCK PIVEN   JENNY POWELL   MEILO SO   MARK ULRIKSE

212 366 1893

MARCO VENTURA   MARY WOODIN   CHRISTOPHER WORMEL

552

JODY HEWGILL

455 W 23RD

NUMBER 8D

NY NY 10011

TELEPHONE

212 366 1893

455 W 23RD

NUMBER 8D

NY NY 10011

TELEPHONE

212 366 1893

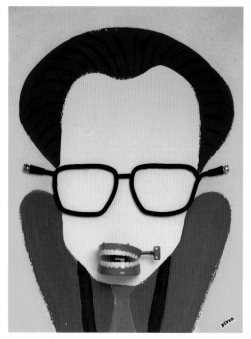

PETER MALONE

DESDEMONA McCANNON

FLORENCE ~ VIEW FROM THE
ARNO.
Desdemona McCannon. 1993

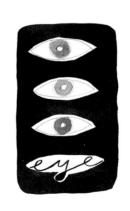

eye

455 W 23RD

NUMBER 8D

NY NY 10011

TELEPHONE

212 366 1893

SALLY HEFLIN
& THE ARTWORKS

555

455 W 23RD

NUMBER 8D

NY NY 10011

TELEPHONE

212 366 1893

CHRISTIAN BIRMINGHAM

SALLY HEFLIN & THE ARTWORKS

ANDREW DAVIDSON

455 W 23RD

NUMBER 8D

NY NY 10011

TELEPHONE

212 366 1893

455 W 23RD

NUMBER 8D

NY NY 10011

TELEPHONE

212 366 1893

MARK ULRIKSEN

455 W 23RD

NUMBER 8D

NY NY 10011

TELEPHONE

212 366 1893

JENNY POWELL

MARY WOODIN

455 W 23RD

NUMBER 8D

NY NY 10011

TELEPHONE

212 366 1893

SALLY HEFLIN & THE ARTWORKS

CHRISTOPHER WORMELL

455 W 23RD

NUMBER 8D

NY NY 10011

TELEPHONE

212 366 1893

SALLY HEFLIN & THE ARTWORKS

455 W 23RD

NUMBER 8D

NY NY 10011

TELEPHONE

212 366 1893

SOPHIE ALLPORT

PENNY DANN

ANNIKA NELSON

455 W 23RD

NUMBER 8D

NY NY 10011

TELEPHONE

212 366 1893

455 W 23RD

NUMBER 8D

NY NY 10011

TELEPHONE

212 366 1893

SARAH McMENEMY

ANTON MORRIS

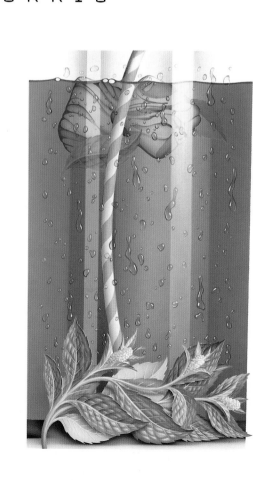

MARCO VENTURA

455 W 23RD

NUMBER 8D

NY NY 10011

TELEPHONE

212 366 1893

455 W 23RD

NUMBER 8D

NY NY 10011

TELEPHONE

212 366 1893

SALLY HEFLIN & THE ARTWORKS

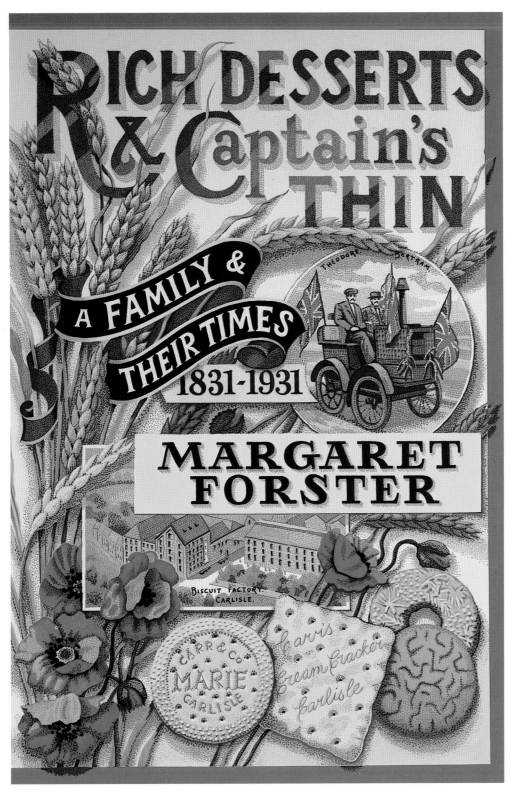

455 W 23RD

NUMBER 8D

NY NY 10011

TELEPHONE

212 366 1893

455 W 23RD

NUMBER 8D

NY NY 10011

TELEPHONE

212 366 1893

CHARLOTTE KNOX

JOHN LAWRENCE

MATTHEW COOK

Back Street, Abbotsbury, Dorset.

455 W 23RD

NUMBER 8D

NY NY 10011

TELEPHONE

212 366 1893

SALLY HEFLIN
& THE ARTWORKS

ZOKA

impetuous

BeefFranks

Orpheus

Fall Festival

Italian

setting every table

Waterbrook

STUDIO (206) 340-9506
Fax 340-9507

Expressive lettering & calligraphic illustration. Clients include: HBO, Harcourt Brace, Harper/Collins, Doubleday, Scott Foresman, Kimberly Clark, Landor Associates, H.W. Lay, Holland America.

Represented on the East Coast by Christine Goodman
Phone: (212) 691-2667

STUDIO (206) 340-9506
Fax 340-9507

BRYAN PETERSON

To see
samples of
Bryan's
digital work,
turn to
Workbook 19

MUNRO
GOODMAN

ARTIST
REPRESENTATIVES

NEW YORK 212.691.2667 FAX 212.633.1844
CHICAGO 312.321.1336 FAX 312.321.1350

MIKE KASUN

NEW YORK 212.691.2667 **FAX** 212.633.1844
CHICAGO 312.321.1336 **FAX** 312.321.1350

MUNRO
GOODMAN

ARTIST
REPRESENTATIVES

Douglas Klauba

NEW YORK 212.691.2667 FAX 212.633.1844
CHICAGO 312.321.1336 FAX 312.321.1350

GREG HARGREAVES

NEW YORK 212.691.2667 FAX 212.633.1844
CHICAGO 312.321.1336 FAX 312.321.1350

MARK CHICKINELLI

NEW YORK 212.691.2667 FAX 212.633.1844
CHICAGO 312.321.1336 FAX 312.321.1350

TOM FOTY

TATJANA KRIZMANIC

NEW YORK 212.691.2667 FAX 212.633.1844
CHICAGO 312.321.1336 FAX 312.321.1350

SALLY WERN COMPORT

NEW YORK 212.691.2667 FAX 212.633.1844

BEN GARVIE

NEW YORK 212.691.2667 FAX 212.633.1844
CHICAGO 312.321.1336 FAX 312.321.1350

MALCOLM FARLEY

NEW YORK 212.691.2667 FAX 212.633.1844
CHICAGO 312.321.1336 FAX 312.321.1350

MUNRO
GOODMAN

ARTIST
REPRESENTATIVES

CHRIS SHEBAN

E.W. INMAN
Artists' Representative

Affiliate · Munro Goodman · Chicago
Contact Emily at 312.321.1336 · Fax 312.321.1350

JEFF BRICE

Kolea Baker Artists Representative

2814 NW 72nd Street   Seattle WA 98117   ph/206.784.1136   fax/206.784.1171   http://www.kolea.com/

Kolea Baker Artists Representative

2814 NW 72nd Street   Seattle WA 98117   ph/206.784.1136   fax/206.784.1171   http://www.kolea.com/

Kolea Baker Artists Representative

2814 NW 72nd Street   Seattle WA 98117   ph/206.784.1136   fax/206.784.1171   http://www.kolea.com/

JERE SMITH

Kolea Baker Artists Representative

2814 NW 72nd Street   Seattle WA 98117   ph/206.784.1136   fax/206.784.1171   http://www.kolea.com/

Kolea Baker Artists Representative

2814 NW 72nd Street   Seattle WA 98117   ph/206.784.1136   fax/206.784.1171   http://www.kolea.com/

DON BAKER

DON BAKER

GEORGE ABE

Kolea Baker Artists Representative

2814 NW 72nd Street   Seattle WA 98117   ph/206.784.1136   fax/206.784.1171   http://www.kolea.com/

GEORGE ABE

Kolea Baker Artists Representative

2814 NW 72nd Street   Seattle WA 98117   ph/206.784.1136   fax/206.784.1171   http://www.kolea.com/

ROY WIEMANN

HIRO KIMURA

J O H N   M A T T O S

CLARE JETT AND ASSOCIATES ✈ **502-228-9427** ✈ **FAX 502-228-8857** ✈ **WWW.WIN.NET/JETTREPS**

DAVE JONASON

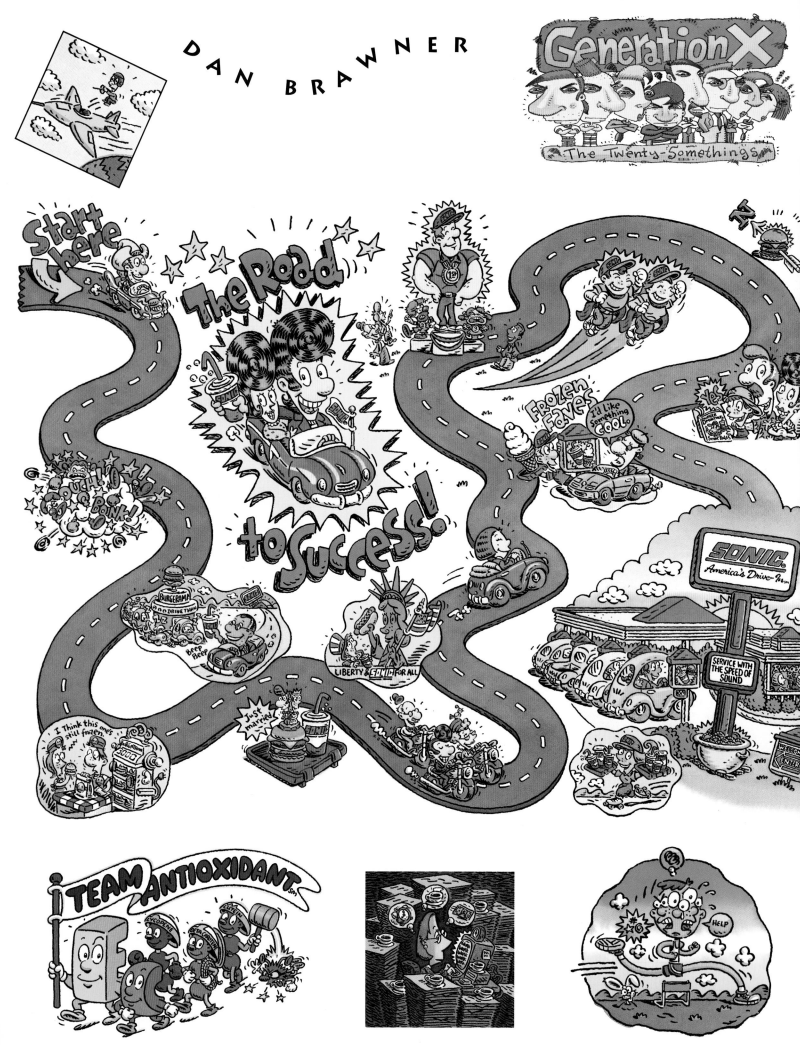

ROBERT FELKER

ANTONIO CANGEMI

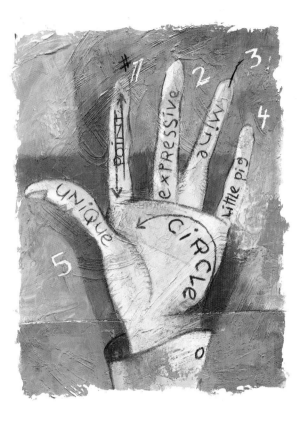

CLAUDIA HAMMER

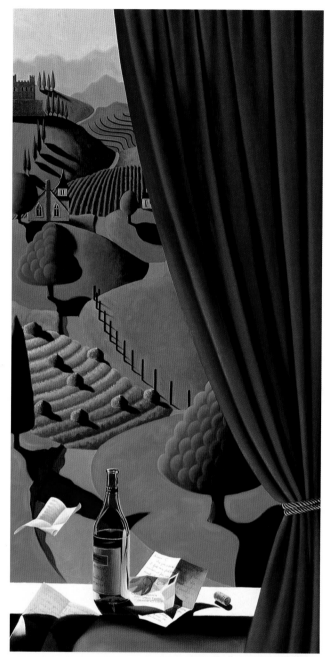

CLARE JETT AND ASSOCIATES ✈ 502-228-9427 ✈ FAX 502-228-8857 ✈ WWW.WIN.NET/JETTREPS

ANNETTE CABLE

the "air" of my garden

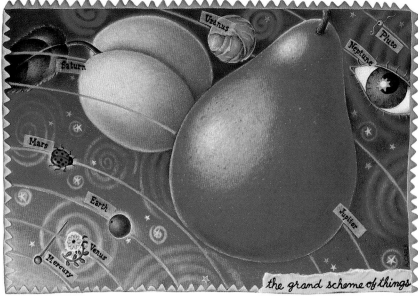

the grand scheme of things

CLARE JETT AND ASSOCIATES ✈ 502-228-9427 ✈ FAX 502-228-8857 ✈ WWW.WIN.NET/JETTREPS

MARK CABLE

STUDIO
405-525-6676

JULIA LAPINE

tel 773 935-8840   fax 773 935-6191

KAREN BELL

CAROLYN POTTS & ASSOCIATES

tel 773 935-8840   fax 773 935-6191

RHONDA VOO

SPRING

CELEBRATIONS

CAROLYN POTTS & ASSOCIATES

tel 773 935-8840   fax 773 935-6191

barbara
KELLEY

In Chicago & Midwest
Represented by
Joni Tuki
(312) 787-6826

IRMELI HOLMBERG

280 madison ave

new york, ny 10016

IRMELI HOLMBERG

REPRESENTATIVE

tel (212) 545-9155

fax (212) 545-9462

www.spar.org/holmberg

IRE

 IR

 ATER

 ARTH

peter
DeFREITAS

tina bela
L I M E R

david
LANTZ

lynne **RIDING**

josef **BELLA**

john **NELSON**

claire **TAGLIANETTI**

meredith **NIEVES**

melanie **BARNES**

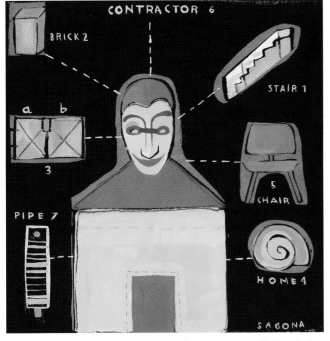

marina **SAGONA**

linda **SCHIWALL**

DAVID TILLINGHAST

PHONE : 626-403-0991   1003 DIAMOND AVENUE • SUITE 200 • SOUTH PASADENA • 91030   FAX: 626-403-0993

REPRESENTED ON THE WEST COAST BY COREY GRAHAM REPRESENTS 415-956-4750

WWW.COREYGRAHAMREPS.COM   WWW.SHOWCASE.COM   E-MAIL: CGR@SLIP.NET

DAVID TILLINGHAST

1003 DIAMOND AVENUE • SUITE 200 • SOUTH PASADENA • 91030   FAX: 626-403-0993   PHONE : 626-403-0991

REPRESENTED ON THE WEST COAST BY COREY GRAHAM REPRESENTS 415-956-4750

WWW.COREYGRAHAMREPS.COM   WWW.SHOWCASE.COM   E-MAIL: CGR@SLIP.NET

623

Matt Manley represented on the west coast by *Corey Graham Represents*

phone 415.956.4750 fax 415.391.6104 website www.coreygrahamreps.com studio 616.459.7595

Joel Nakamura

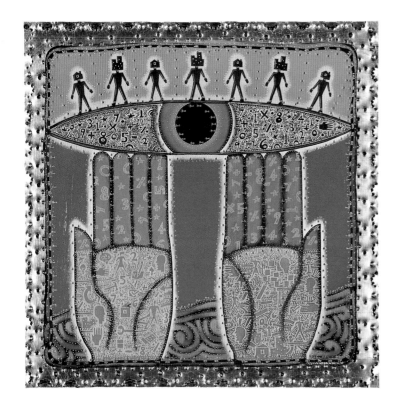

Joel Nakamura   Studio • 505 • 989 • 1404
•••
in San Francisco • call Corey Graham
415 • 956 • 4750

DEBRA HARDESTY

1017 VALLEJO WAY   SACRAMENTO, CA 95818   TEL 916.446.1824   FAX 916.446.5661

REPRESENTED ON THE WEST COAST BY COREY GRAHAM REPRESENTS   415.956.4750

Andrea Brooks

212.633.1477

Hungarian
Sweet Chile
mild and sweet

On the west coast call:
Corey Graham
Tel: 415.956.4750
Fax: 415.391.6104

Gerber Baby Food

To view more work:
www.showcase.com or www.coreygrahamreps.com

631

Weighing trade-offs in creating your investment mix.

Frank Ansley
415•989•9614
Fax•989•9630

Animation Reel Available.

Represented by•Corey Graham•415•956•4750 Fax•415•391•6104

JOE LeMONNIER

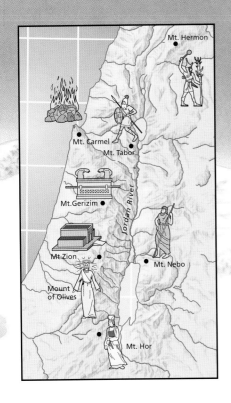

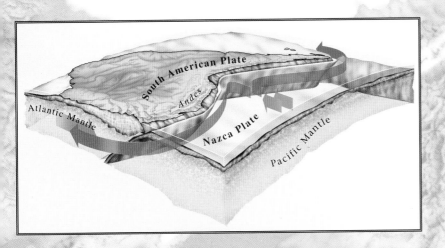

Melissa Turk
THE ARTIST NETWORK

phone (914) 368-8606 / fax (914) 368-8608   9 babbling brook lane / suffern, new york 10901

DREW·BROOK·CORMACK ASSOC.

Melissa Turk
THE ARTIST NETWORK

phone (914) 368-8606 / fax (914) 368-8608   9 babbling brook lane / suffern, new york 10901

WENDY SMITH·GRISWOLD

MelissaTurk
THE ARTIST NETWORK

phone (914) 368-8606 / fax (914) 368-8608   9 babbling brook lane / suffern, new york 10901

BRIDGET STARR TAYLOR

FRIENDS

MARIE

OUT TO PAINT THE TOWN

LOS ANGELES 213.934.3395   CHICAGO 312.222.0337

PAINTING BY DAVID WILLARDSON

CHRIS CONSANI

RITA MARIE • RODNEY RAY
Los Angeles 213/934-3395 Fax 213/936-2757
Chicago 312/222-0337 Fax 773/883-0375

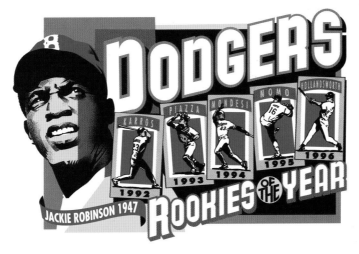

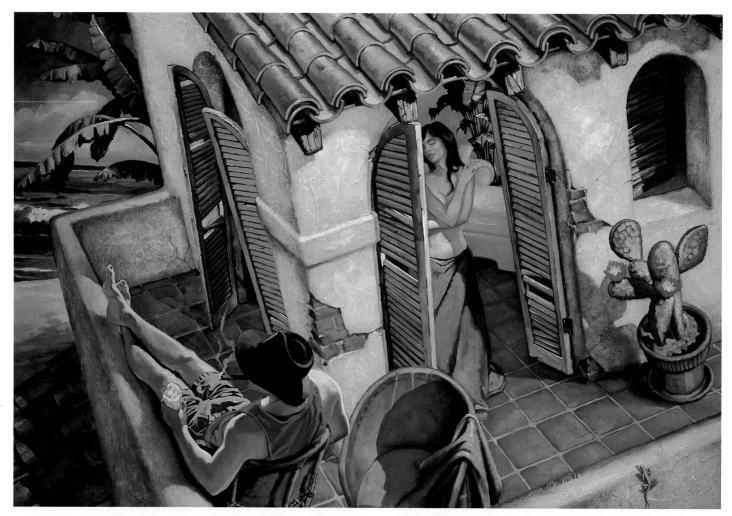

RITA MARIE • RODNEY RAY
Los Angeles 213/934-3395 Fax 213/936-2757
Chicago 312/222-0337 Fax 773/883-0375

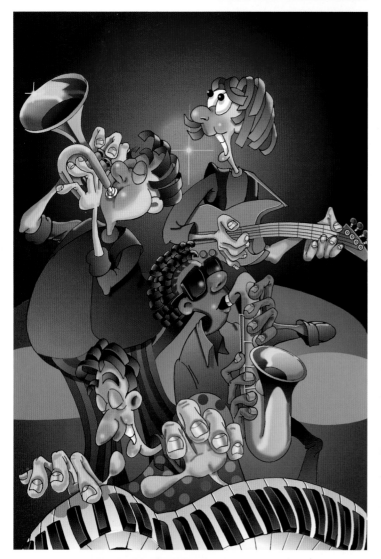

RITA MARIE • RODNEY RAY
Los Angeles 213/934-3395 Fax 213/936-2757
Chicago 312/222-0337 Fax 773/883-0375

RITA MARIE • RODNEY RAY
Los Angeles 213/934-3395 Fax 213/936-2757
Chicago 312/222-0337 Fax 773/883-0375

relic (rel´ik), *n*. 1. illustrator. 2. muralist. 3. contemporary logo designer. 4. graffiti artist-.pulling no punches to get a point across. **A Modern Cla**

RITA MARIE
RODNEY RAY

Los Angeles (213) 934-3395 fax (213) 936-2757
Chicago (312) 222-0337 fax (773) 883-0375

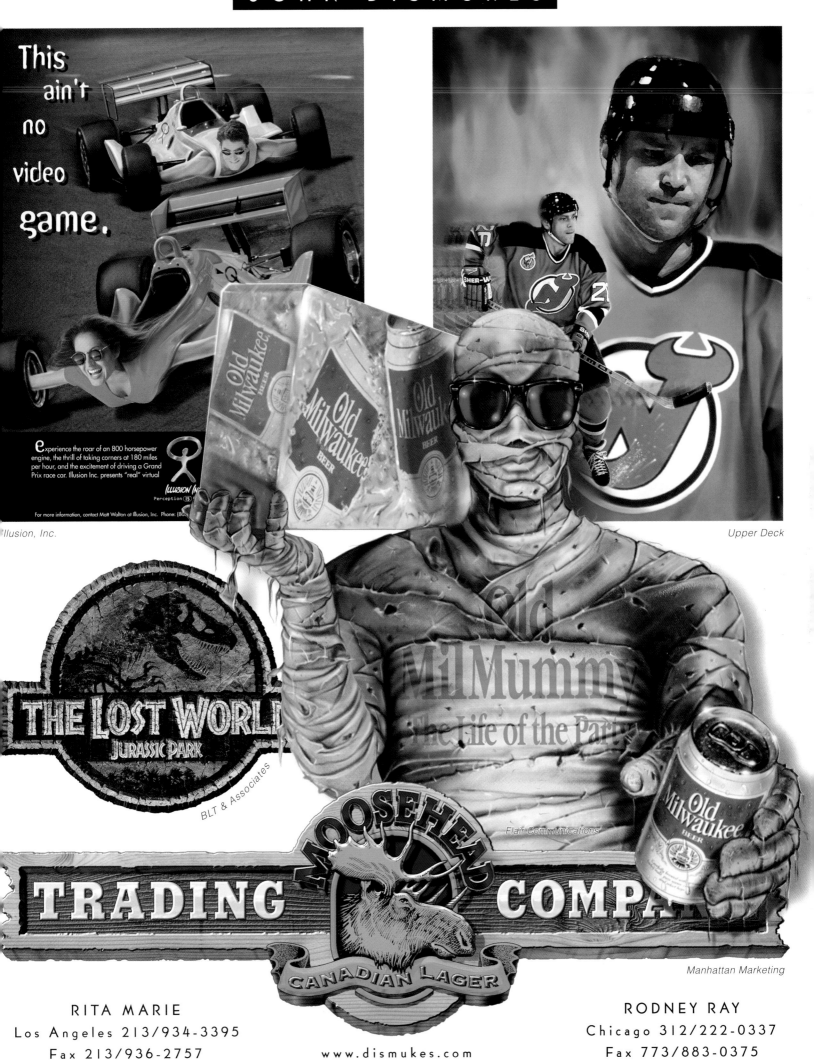

Lilla ROGERS

www.theispot.com/artist/lrogers

Cedus Le Sucre

Profiles Magazine

Teach your children Life is gentle.

Teach your children Life is short.

Rogers

HUNTERS OF THE SKY now at the Academy of Natural Sciences through May 4, 1997. And don't miss our live butterflies exhibit.

Hunters of the Sky was produced by The Science Museum of Minnesota and is presented at the Academy through the generous sponsorship of Sunoco. **SUNOCO**

Academy of Natural Sciences/Earle Palmer Brown

6 PARKER ROAD ARLINGTON MA 02174

LILLA ROGERS STUDIO

TEL 781 641 2787 FAX 781 641 2244

Diane **BIGDA**

www.theispot.com/artist/bigda

Represented by
LILLA ROGERS

Autumn Leaves Giftware

McGraw Hill

American Way Magazine

6 PARKER ROAD ARLINGTON MA 02174

LILLA
ROGERS
STUDIO

TEL 781 641 2787   FAX 781 641 2244

Makiko AZAKAMI

Represented by
LILLA ROGERS

Creo

Taihoh Co. Supermarket

DINER
WELCOME   24 hrs.

PARKING
IN
REAR

OPEN

HOT DOG

COFFEE

PAPER TOY

Goken Publishing Co.

6 PARKER ROAD ARLINGTON MA 02174

LILLA
ROGERS
STUDIO

TEL 781 641 2787   FAX 781 641 2244

Kim DEMARCO

In
India
we looked up at the mountains
from the roof of Neemrana
palace

We rode
bikes and camels to a
Berber camp
in the dunes of
Morocco

Frank Viva/Viva Dolan/Butterfield & Robinson

American OnLine

We joined the
crowds
waving their Palio banners
on Siena's main square in
Tuscany

Butterfield & Robinson

Quickly!

We've made our final
seasonal markdowns.
40 to 60% off
regular prices for
men and women.

BARNEYS
NEW YORK

MADISON AVENUE AND SIXTY-FIRST STREET 212 826 8900
SEVENTH AVENUE AND SEVENTEENTH STREET 212 929 9000

Barneys

TokYo
GiRL

6 PARKER ROAD ARLINGTON MA 02174

TEL 781 641 2787   FAX 781 641 2244

British GQ

Quest Magazine

Brazn

Ghislaine Dunant

Book-of-the-Month Club

Ann BOYAJIAN

www.theispot.com/artist/boyajian

Represented by
LILLA ROGERS

Parents Magazine

Glamour Magazine

6 PARKER ROAD ARLINGTON MA 02174

LILLA ROGERS STUDIO

TEL 781 641 2787   FAX 781 641 2244

Belk Mignogna/UltraFem Annual Report

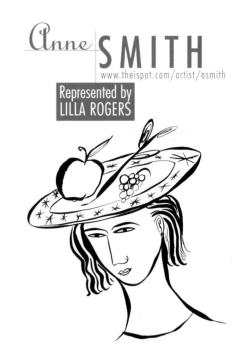

Anne's work for the
UltraFem Annual Report
was recently awarded

"Best Illustrated
Annual Report"
in Print's AR100

Belk Mignogna/UltraFem Annual Report

Diablo Magazine

Susy Pilgrim WATERS

Represented by
LILLA ROGERS

6 PARKER ROAD ARLINGTON MA 02174

LILLA
ROGERS
STUDIO

TEL 781 641 2787   FAX 781 641 2244

Harvard University Press

American Demographics Magazine/Dow Jones

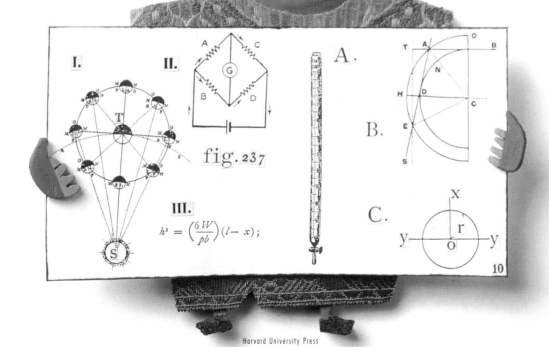
Harvard University Press

6 PARKER ROAD ARLINGTON MA 02174

LILLA
ROGERS
STUDIO

TEL 781 641 2787 FAX 781 641 2244

TIM
O'BRIEN

LOTT
REPRESENTATIVES

60 E. 42 ST. #1146 • N.Y., N.Y. 10165 • (212) 953-7088

ERIC J.W.
LEE

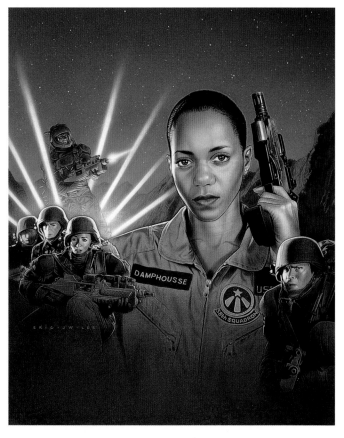

LOTT
REPRESENTATIVES

60 E. 42 ST. #1146 • N.Y., N.Y. 10165 • (212) 953-7088

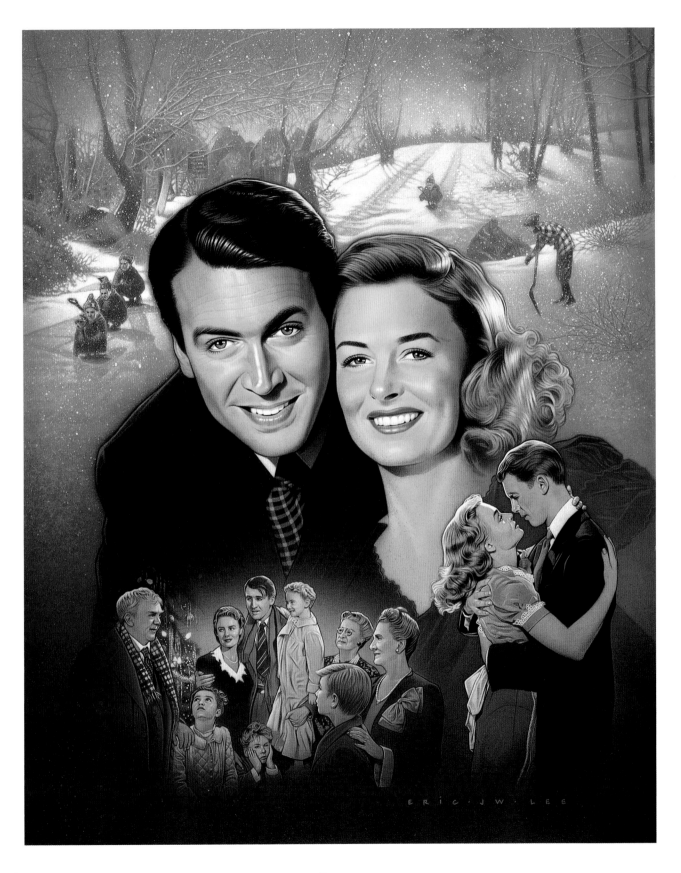

BARBARA
TYLER

LOTT
REPRESENTATIVES

60 E. 42 ST. #1146 • N.Y., N.Y. 10165 • (212) 953-7088

E D
KURTZMAN

LOTT
REPRESENTATIVES

60 E. 42 ST. #1146 • N.Y., N.Y. 10165 • (212) 953-7088

MARK
NAGATA

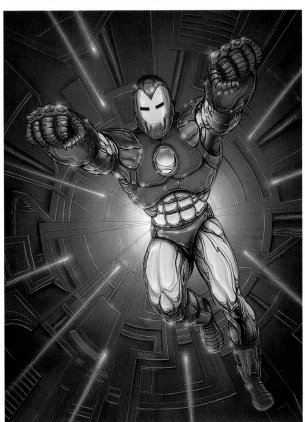

LOTT
REPRESENTATIVES

60 E. 42 ST. #1146 • N.Y., N.Y. 10165 • (212) 953-7088

ART VALERO

SCOTT NASH

JENNIFER THERMES

LINDA BRONSON

REPRESENTED BY LEIGHTON & COMPANY CALL 978 921 0887 FAX 978 921 0223

http://www.leightonreps.com

ANNETTE KRAUS

DIGITAL ILLUSTRATION

AUGUST STEIN

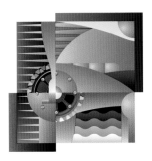

STEVE MEEK

ROB BOLSTER

TOTALLY DIGITAL ILLUSTRATIONS

Paul Watson

Kim Fujiwara

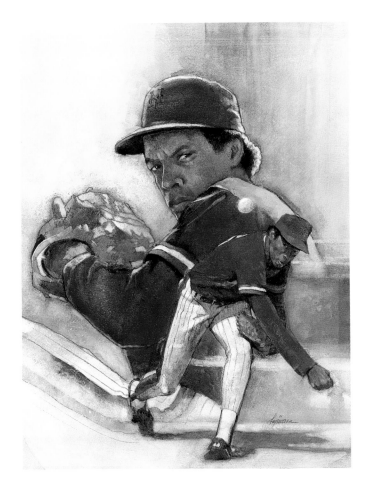

Kathryn Adams

toronto 416-367-2446   312-663-5506 chicago
new york 212-643-0896   213-688-7428 los angeles
southeast usa 904-747-8415   0-186-543-5654 united kingdom

artist representatives - call for portfolios

Dave Whamond

toronto 416-367-2446 312-663-5506 chicago
new york 212-643-0896 213-688-7428 los angeles
southeast usa 904-747-8415 0-186-543-5654 united kingdom

artist representatives - call for portfolios

Anne Stanley

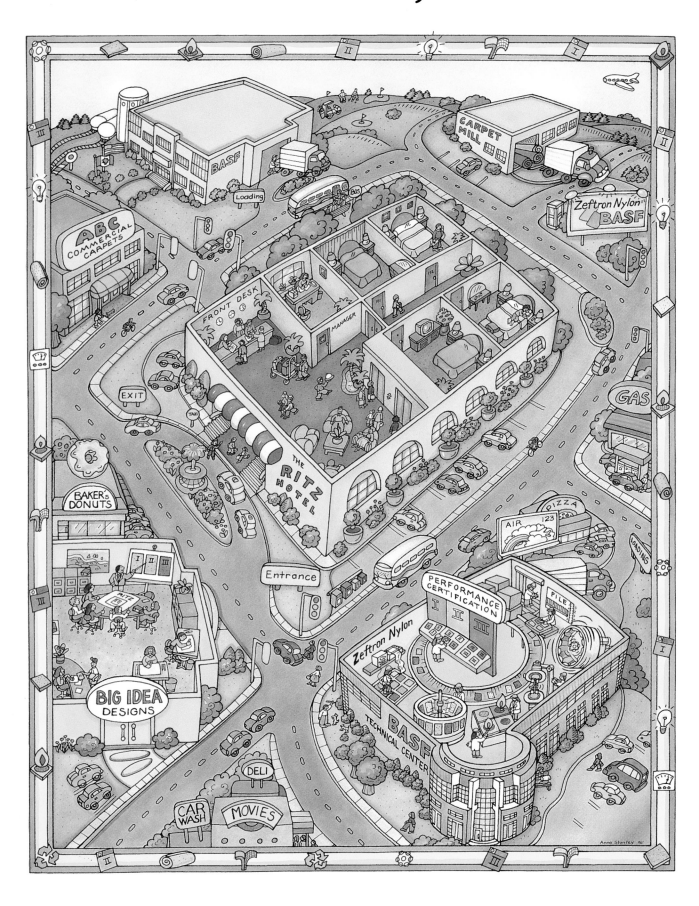

toronto 416-367-2446
new york 212-643-0896
southeast usa 904-747-8415

312-663-5506 chicago
213-688-7428 los angeles
0-186-543-5654 united kingdom

artist representatives - call for portfolios

Scot Ritchie

Bob Daly

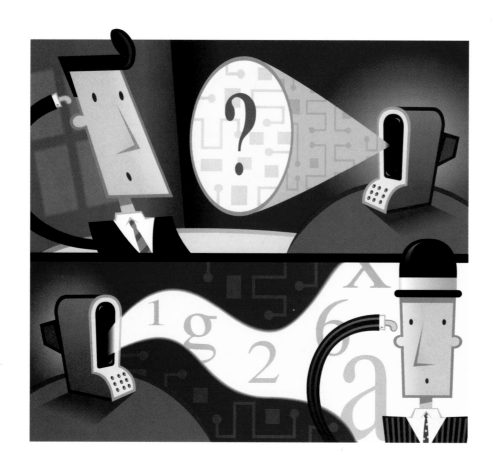

Rose Zgodzinski

Where Omega-3s May Help

Potential benefits of omega-3s reach from head to toe

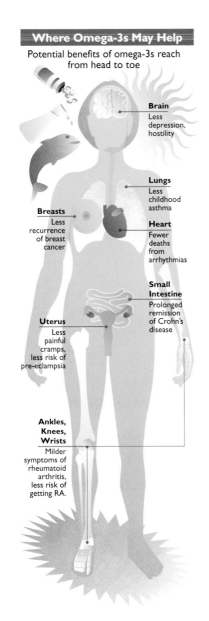

Brain
Less depression, hostility

Lungs
Less childhood asthma

Breasts
Less recurrence of breast cancer

Heart
Fewer deaths from arrhythmias

Small Intestine
Prolonged remission of Crohn's disease

Uterus
Less painful cramps, less risk of pre-eclampsia

Ankles, Knees, Wrists
Milder symptoms of rheumatoid arthritis, less risk of getting RA.

Do you have an area for counselling?

57.6% Yes

25.7% No, but plan to within 12 months

16.7% No

WHO SELLS THE MOST CHOCOLATE BARS?

Single chocolate bar sales volume by retail category

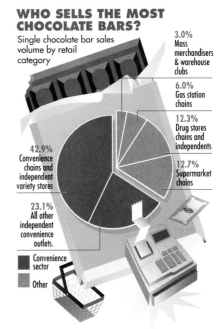

3.0% Mass merchandisers & warehouse clubs

6.0% Gas station chains

12.3% Drug stores chains and independents

12.7% Supermarket chains

42.9% Convenience chains and independent variety stores

23.1% All other independent convenience outlets.

- Convenience sector
- Other

Our support for small business continues to grow

New small business accounts
In billions of dollars

Sept. '95	$11.1
Dec. '95	$11.3
March '96	$11.4
June '96	$11.5

$10 $11

WHAT'S IN A PC's PRICE?
Dell Dimension P166V
(March 1997)

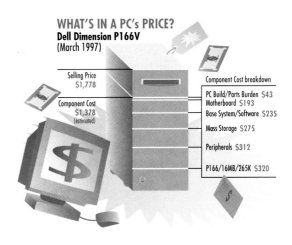

Selling Price $1,778

Component Cost $1,378 (estimated)

Component Cost breakdown
PC Build/Parts Burden $43
Motherboard $193
Base System/Software $235
Mass Storage $275
Peripherals $312
P166/16MB/265K $320

toronto 416-367-2446
new york 212-643-0896
southeast usa 904-747-8415

312-663-5506 chicago
213-688-7428 los angeles
0-186-543-5654 united kingdom

artist representatives - call for portfolios

S.I. International

ART FOR ENTERTAINMENT

S.I. International
43 East 19th Street
New York, NY 10003
Tel. (212) 254.4996
Fax (212) 995.0911
Internet Address:
http://www.si-i.com

ILLUSTRATION & DESIGN LAYOUT
BY CK DESIGN
CHARLES KUHTIC & MIKE KENNY

TOM LAPADULA

CAROLYN BRACKEN

FERNANDO GUELL © DISNEY

MARK MARDAROSIAN © DISNEY

BRUCE EAGLE

KAREN BAUMANN

S.I. International

ART FOR ENTERTAINMENT

S.I. International
43 East 19th Street
New York, NY 10003
Tel. (212) 254.4996
Fax (212) 995.0911
Internet Address:
http://www.si-i.com

ILLUSTRATION & DESIGN LAYOUT
BY CK DESIGN
CHARLES KUHTIC & MIKE KENNY

THOMPSON BROS. © FOX

ISIDRE MONES © MARVEL COMICS

BOB OSTROM

CK DESIGN / CHARES KUHTIC

S.I. International

ART FOR ENTERTAINMENT

S.I. International
43 East 19th Street
New York, NY 10003
Tel. (212) 254.4996
Fax (212) 995.0911
Internet Address:
http://www.si-i.com

ILLISTRATION & DESIGN LAYOUT
BY CK DESIGN
CHARLES KUHTIC & MIKE KENNY

FRED MARVIN

MEL GRANT

JOSE-MARIA MIRALLES

JORDI TORRES

GABRIEL PICART

JOHN KURTZ © DISNEY

S.I. International

ART FOR ENTERTAINMENT

S.I. International
43 East 19th Street
New York, NY 10003
Tel. (212) 254.4996
Fax (212) 995.0911
Internet Address:
http://www.si-i.com

ILLUSTRATION & DESIGN LAYOUT
BY CK DESIGN
CHARLES KUHTIC & MIKE KENNY

ARISTIDES RUIZ

JANE KURISU

GONZALEZ VICENTE © MATTEL

DAVID CHRISTENSEN

SEGUNDO GARCIA

TED ENIK

FRANC MATEU
© HANNA BARBERA

S.I. International

ART FOR ENTERTAINMENT

S.I. International
43 East 19th Street
New York, NY 10003
Tel. (212) 254.4996
Fax (212) 995.0911
Internet Address:
http://www.si-i.com

ILLISTRATION & DESIGN LAYOUT
BY CK DESIGN
CHARLES KUHTIC & MIKE KENNY

NANCY STEVENSON © DISNEY

ROBBIN CUDDY © DISNEY

STEVE HASKAMP

ALLEN DAVIS

CARLOS NINE

CARDONA STUDIO © DISNEY

S.I. International

ART FOR ENTERTAINMENT

S.I. International
43 East 19th Street
New York, NY 10003
Tel. (212) 254.4996
Fax (212) 995.0911
Internet Address:
http://www.si-i.com

ILLISTRATION & DESIGN LAYOUT
BY CK DESIGN
CHARLES KUHTIC & MIKE KENNY

RICHARD COURTNEY

HOLLY HANNON

JIM DURK

FRANCESC RIGOL © DISNEY

JOSIE YEE © DISNEY

CK DESIGN © MIKE KENNY

SERRAT-SANS © BLUEBIRD

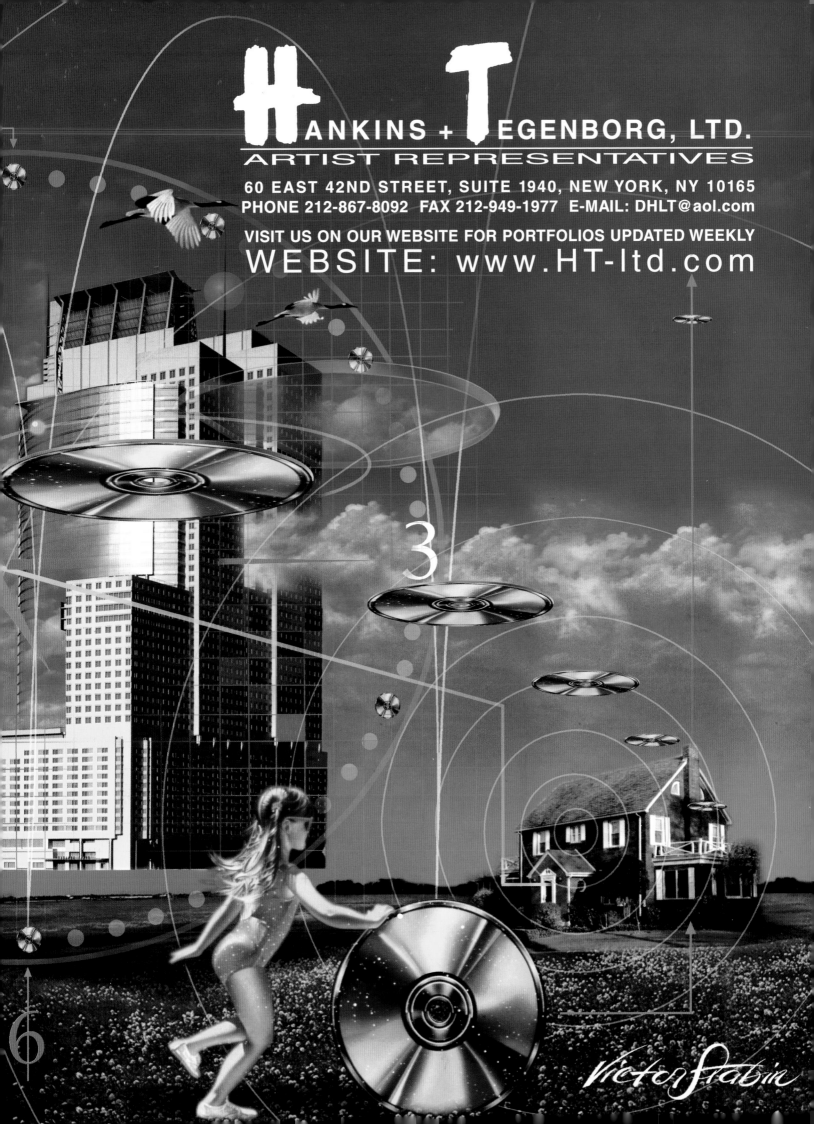

Seagram's COOLERS Brings you SIZZLING SAVINGS!

Get Your Groove On

Daphne McCormack

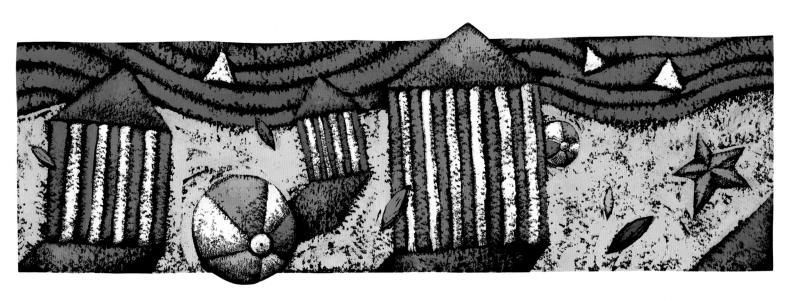

Sharron O'Neil

© Sharron G. O'Neil
1989
California Buckeye

© Sharon O'Neil Nov. 1996 Iceberg Rose at Season's End   California

Bill Firestone

MARY ROSS

Recycle

The Coast is Clear

Mozzarella's
American Bar.

A Star is Born

DIANE VARNEY

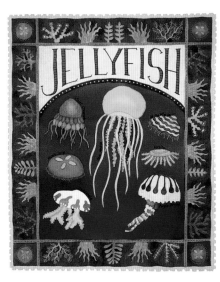

RITA GATLIN REPRESENTS

USA 800.924.7881 • SF 415.924.7881 • FAX 415.924.7891 • www.ritareps.com

WHITNEY SHERMAN

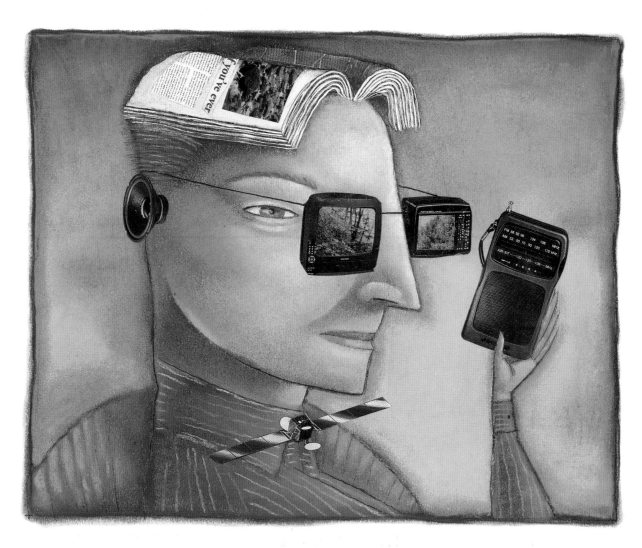

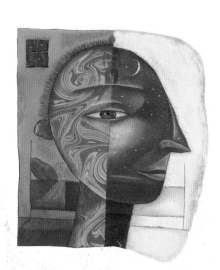

RITA GATLIN REPRESENTS

USA 800.924.7881 • SF 415.924.7881 • FAX 415.924.7891 • www.ritareps.com

RUSS CHARPENTIER

produced for Sears

concept package design

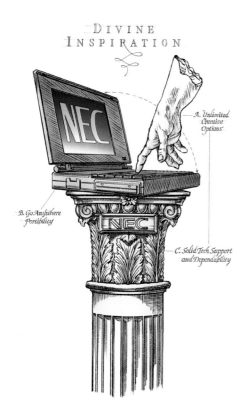

U.S. Airways Magazine

TOM HENNESSY

RITA GATLIN REPRESENTS

USA 800.924.7881 · **SF** 415.924.7881 · **FAX** 415.924.7891 · www.ritareps.com

702

London
Paris   Costa Rica
Miami

Ibiza

Milan
Timbuktu

TOP
10

Mirror mirror on the wall,

who is the poodliest of all?

(SHOE)

SUSAN AND CO

ARTIST REPRESENTATIVE

PHONE 206 232 7873

FAX 206 232 7908

JONATHAN COMBS

REPRESENTED BY RON SWEET

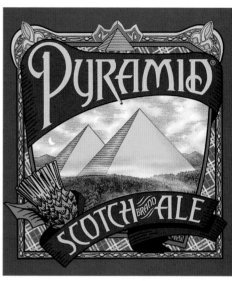

WILL NELSON

REPRESENTED BY RON SWEET

ROBERT EVANS

REPRESENTED BY RON SWEET

Arciero

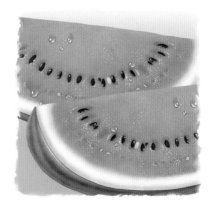  

Naked Juice

RACHAEL McCAMPBELL

REPRESENTED BY RON SWEET

DEREK MUELLER

REPRESENTED BY RON SWEET

See portfolio on line at www.showcase.com

SWEET REPRESENTS   415 433 1222   FAX 415 433 9560   716 MONTGOMERY STREET   SAN FRANCISCO CA 94111

STEVEN NOBLE

REPRESENTED BY RON SWEET

STOCK EXCHANGE

JIM LILIE 415 441·4384   FAX 415 395·9809

Slider

Knuckle Ball

DUGALD STERMER   REPRESENTED BY JIM LILIE   415.441.4384

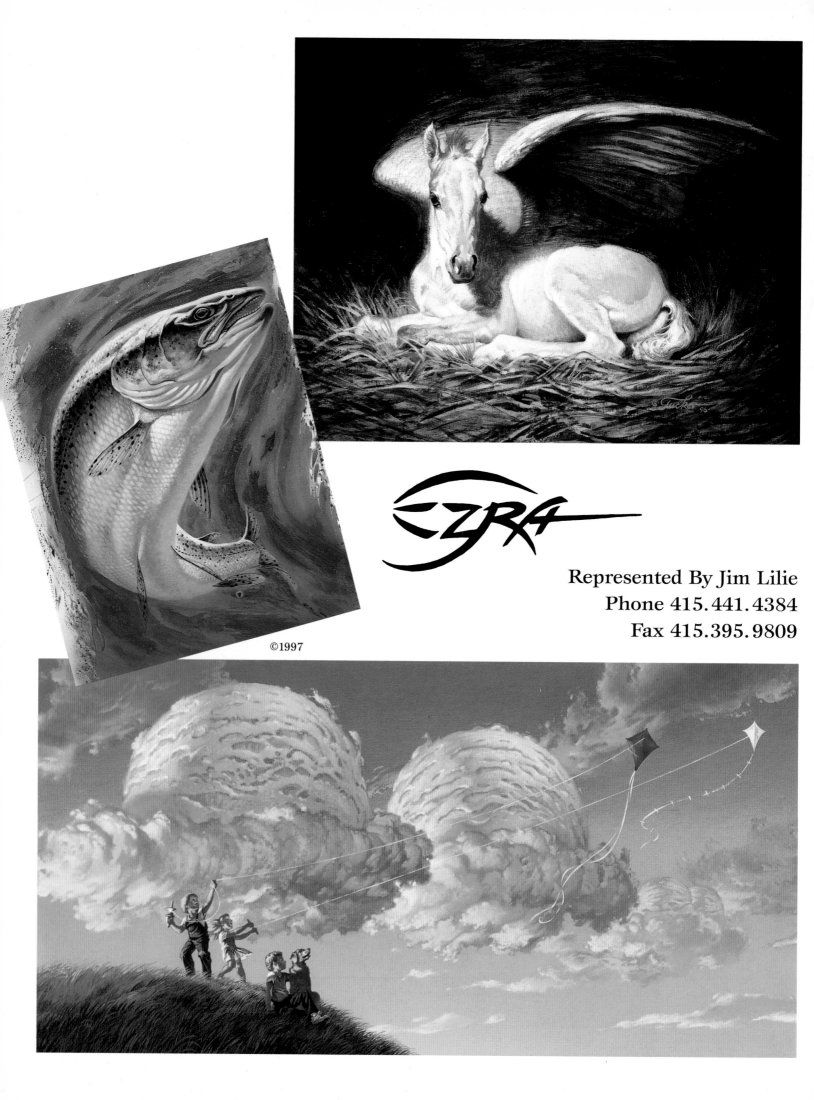

EZRA

Represented By Jim Lilie
Phone 415.441.4384
Fax 415.395.9809

©1997

Richard Quan Nguyen
Represented By Jim Lilie
Phone 415.441.4384

©1997

Travis Foster

Represented by Jan Collier (415) 383-9026 (415) 383-9037 fax collierreps.com
Editorial (615) 227-0895

Barbara Banthien

Represented by Jan Collier (415) 383-9026 (415) 383-9037 fax collierreps.com

Rich Borge

Represented by Jan Collier (415) 383-9026 (415) 383-9037 fax collierreps.com
New York and Editorial (212) 262-9823 mindinmotion.com/borge

Raphael Montoliu

christer ERIKSSON

dean**KENNEDY**

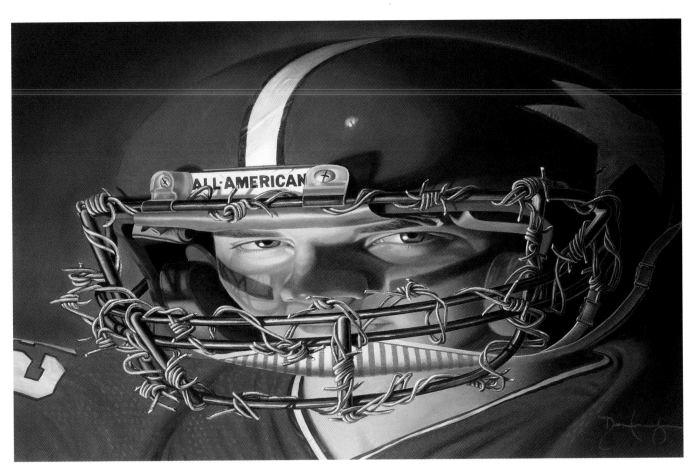

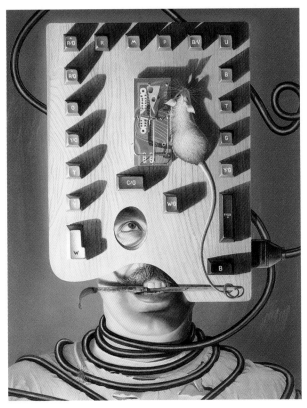

tomWARD

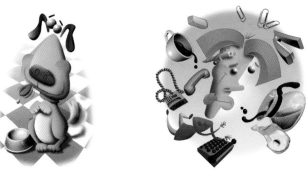

DAN COSGROVE

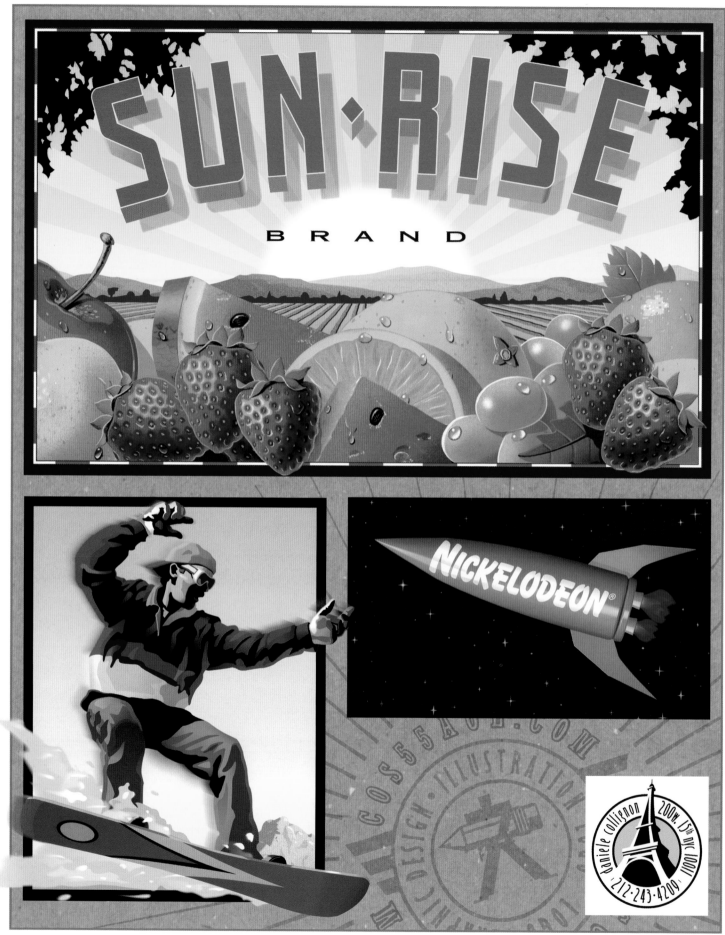

CHICAGO, STUDIO (312) 609-0050

VICKI YIANNIAS

studio 1.305.672.3363   wframpton@aol.com

bill frampton

DANIELE COLLIGNON · 200 W. 15ᵀᴴ NYC 10011 · 212·243·4209

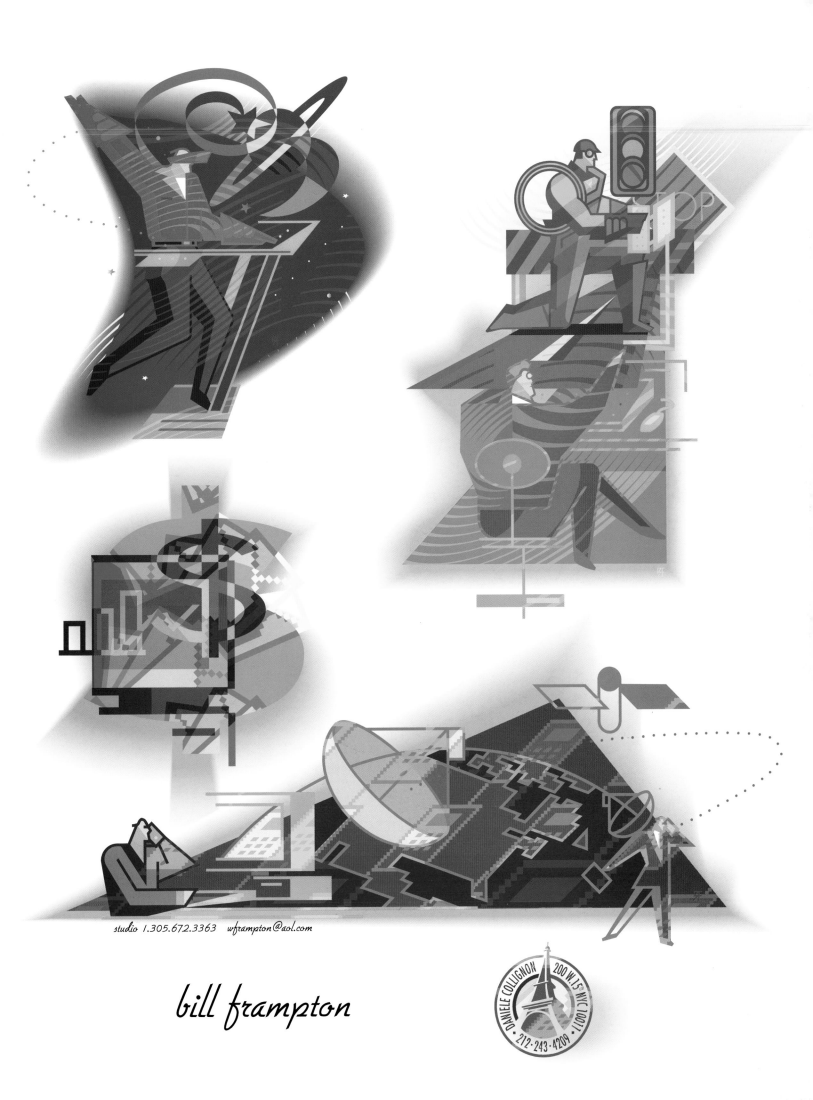

studio 1.305.672.3363 wframpton@aol.com

bill frampton

DANIELE COLLIGNON 200 W.15th NYC 10011
212·243·4209

BRIAN AJHAR

BRIAN AJHAR

PAMELA
KORN

(717) 595-9298   fax (717) 595-9392   http://www.theispot.com/artist/ajhar

JEFF MOORES

COMPUTER ANIMATION AVAILABLE

PAMELA
KORN

(717) 595-9298 fax (717) 595-9392   http://www.theispot.com/artist/moores

PAMELA

KORN

(717) 595-9298   fax (717) 595-9392   http://www.theispot.com/artist/moores

CHRISTOPHER ZACHAROW

ROBERT GOLDSTROM

ROY CARRUTHERS

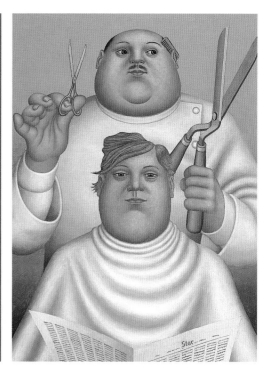

ROBERT GIUSTI

VICTOR JUHASZ

JULIAN ALLEN

THE NEWBORN GROUP

REPRESENTATIVE
JOAN SIGMAN

http://www.zaks.com/
illustrators/newborn
TEL 212•260•6700
FAX 212•260•9600

MARK HESS   DAVID WILCOX   TERESA FASOLINO

JAMES MARSH   JOHN H HOWARD   WILSON M^cLEAN

THE NEWBORN GROUP

REPRESENTATIVE

JOAN SIGMAN

http://www.zaks.com/
illustrators/newborn
TEL 212•260•6700
FAX 212•260•9600

741

Roger Chandler

Sharif Tarabay

represented by John Brewster Creative Services 203.226.4724 *fax* 203.454.9904

CECI BARTELS
ASSOCIATES

3286 Ivanhoe
St.Louis MO 63139
cecicba@stlnet.com

Telephone
314.781.7377

Facsimile
314.781.8017

Chicago
312.786.1560

New York
212.912.1877

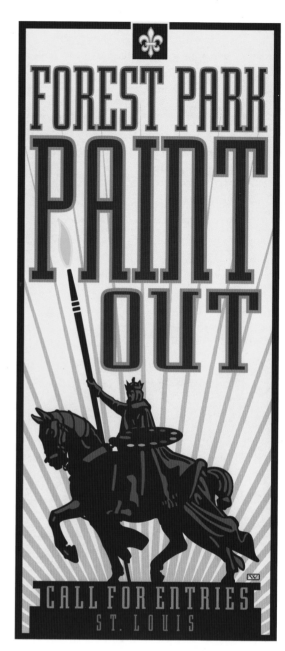

ted **WRIGHT**

CECI BARTELS
ASSOCIATES

3286 Ivanhoe
St. Louis MO 63139
cecicba@stlnet.com

Telephone
314.781.7377

Facsimile
314.781.8017

Chicago
312.786.1560

New York
212.912.1877

lindy
BURNETT

JULIA LA PINE

represented on the west coast by

SHARON DODGE
+ASSOCIATES

ARTIST REPRESENTATIVES Illustrators + Photographers phone 206.284.4701 fax 206.282.3499 web http://www.halcyon.com/dodg

ROBERT BRÜNZ

Portfolio and stock available at http://www.brunz.com   phone 1.800.750.5809 fax 206.467.7216

SHARON DODGE
+ASSOCIATES

ARTIST REPRESENTATIVES   Illustrators + Photographers   phone 206.284.4701   fax 206.282.3499   web http://www.halcyon.com/dodge

Illustrations for
Paul Stuart Stores,
New York
Chicago

PAUL
ZWOLAK

Paul Zwolak
Represented by

Marlena Agency

tel. 212 289 5514, 609 252 9405
fax. 609 252 1949

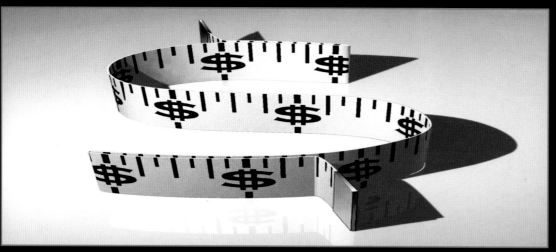

REPRESENTING:

LOUISHENDERSON

BENOIT

REBECCA GIBBON

WILLIAM BRAMHALL

GRETCHEN DOW SIMPSON

WARREN LINN

EDWARD KOREN

Riley Illustration

TERESA SHELLEY AND LETICIA GERMON NEW YORK CITY TEL (212) 989-8770 FAX (212) 989-7892

TERESA SHELLEY AND LETICIA GERMON   NEW YORK CITY   TEL (212) 989-8770   FAX (212) 989-7892

Riley Illustration

REPRESENTING:
BENOIT, WILLIAM BRAMHALL, ISABELLE DERVAUX, JEFFERY FISHER, REBECCA GIBBON, PIERRE LE-TAN, EDWARD KOREN, WARREN LINN, ROBERT ANDREW PARKER, LIZ PYLE, JEAN JACQUES SEMPE, DANNY SHANAHAN, GRETCHEN DOW SIMPSON, PHILIPPE WEISBECKER, & OTHERS

PHILIPPE WEISBECKER

JEFFERY FISHER

DANNY SHANAHAN

PIERRE LE-TAN

LIZ PYLE

ISABELLE DERVAUX

Anne Albrecht, President
Holly Hahn, Co-Vice President
Bob Wolter, Co-Vice President
Chris Glenn, Treasurer
Sharon Langley, Secretary

CHICAGO ARTIST REPRESENTATIVES

Mary Atols
Liz Baugher
Patrice Bockos
Simone Friend
Candace Gelman
Gabrielle Giebels
Lee Hackney
Jim Hanson
Joel Harlib
John Hoffman
Emily Inman
Vince Kamin
Sue Katz
David Montagano
Steve Munro
Linda Shekut
Linda Thomsen
Julie Vargo
Jim Wilson
Jodie Zeitler
Wendy Zunker

312•409•6211

An organization committed to the highest degree of professional service on behalf of photographers, illustrators and film directors for all buyers of art.

Bruck & Moss
Nancy Bruck
(212) 982-6533 • FAX: (212) 358-1586
Eileen Moss
(212) 980-8061 • FAX: (212) 832-8778

Representing

Dave Black

■

Tom Curry

■

Lydia Hess

■

D. B. Johnson

■

Joel Peter Johnson

■

Katie Keller

■

Elizabeth Lada

■

Susan LeVan

■

Malin Lindgren

■

Andre Lucero

■

Adam Niklewicz

■

Rebecca Rüegger

Bruck & Moss
Eileen Moss
(212) 980-8061 • FAX: (212) 832-8778
Nancy Bruck
(212) 982-6533 • FAX: (212) 358-1586

Digital Art

L y d i a   H e s s

Bruck & Moss
Eileen Moss
(212) 980-8061 • FAX: (212) 832-8778
Nancy Bruck
(212) 982-6533 • FAX: (212) 358-1586

Tom Curry

Bruck & Moss
Eileen Moss
(212) 980-8061 • FAX: (212) 832-8778
Nancy Bruck
(212) 982-6533 • FAX: (212) 358-1586

D . B .   J o h n s o n

Bruck & Moss
Nancy Bruck
(212) 982-6533 • FAX: (212) 358-1586
Eileen Moss
(212) 980-8061 • FAX: (212) 832-8778

Elizabeth Lada

Bruck & Moss
Nancy Bruck
(212) 982-6533 • FAX: (212) 358-1586
Eileen Moss
(212) 980-8061 • FAX: (212) 832-8778

A d a m   N i k l e w i c z

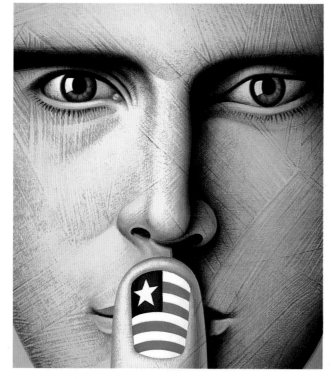

Bruck & Moss
Eileen Moss
(212) 980-8061 • FAX: (212) 832-8778
Nancy Bruck
(212) 982-6533 • FAX: (212) 358-1586

BRUCK & MOSS

Dave Black

Bruck & Moss
Nancy Bruck
(212) 982-6533 • FAX: (212) 358-1586
Eileen Moss
(212) 980-8061 • FAX: (212) 832-8778

Andre Lucero

ruck & Moss
ancy Bruck
12) 982-6533 • FAX: (212) 358-1586
een Moss
12) 980-8061 • FAX: (212) 832-8778

Digital Art

Susan LeVan

Bruck & Moss
Nancy Bruck
(212) 982-6533 • FAX: (212) 358-1586
Eileen Moss
(212) 980-8061 • FAX: (212) 832-8778

Joel Peter Johnson

ruck & Moss
een Moss
12) 980-8061 • FAX: (212) 832-8778
ancy Bruck
12) 982-6533 • FAX: (212) 358-1586

Rebecca Rüegger

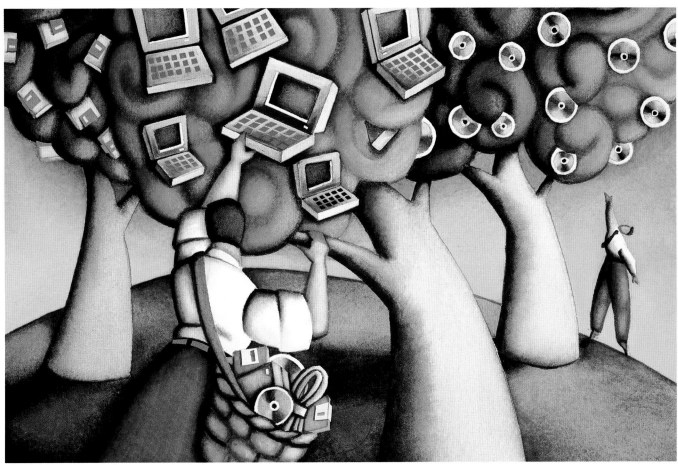

Randall Burg Fine Art
4224 Glencoe Avenue
Marina Del Rey, California 90292
(310) 827-2470, (800) 397-1119
FAX: (310) 827-8890
e-mail: rbartguy@earthlink.net
www.christinademuseeworld.com

Christina De Musée

Harcourt Brace Textbook Publishers
Supergrafx, Inc.
Spangler & Associates
Boulevard Magazine
Exito! Magazine
Government of Granada
Wizard & Genius Idealdecor Ag

Men's Fitness Magazine
Paramount Pictures
Universal Studios
Canyon Cove Films
L.A. Weekly Magazine
Light Entertainment
Cortina Entertainment

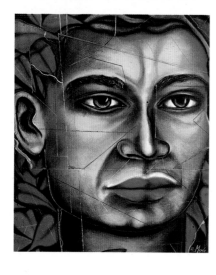

CHRISTINA DE MUSÉE

310 827 2470

Carol Chislovsky Design, Inc.
53 Broadway, Suite 1201
New York, New York 10003
(212) 677-9100
FAX: (212) 353-0954

CHISLOVSKY

JULIE PACE   Digital Illustrator

Carol Chislovsky Design, Inc.
853 Broadway, Suite 1201
New York, New York 10003
(212) 677-9100
FAX: (212) 353-0954

CHISLOVSKY

Daniels & Daniels

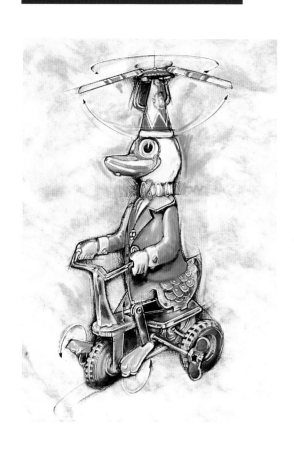

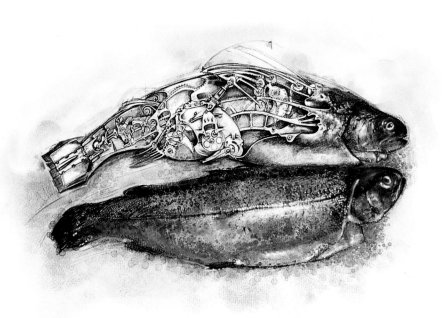

Carol Chislovsky Design, Inc.
53 Broadway, Suite 1201
New York, New York 10003
(212) 677-9100
FAX: (212) 353-0954

CHISLOVSKY

Daniels & Daniels

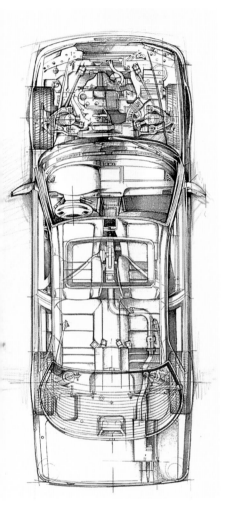

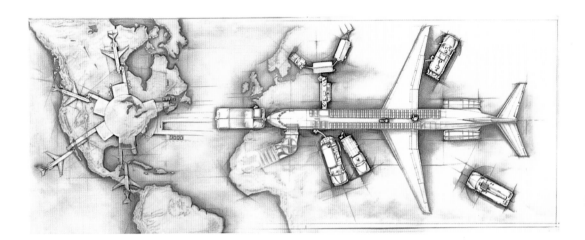

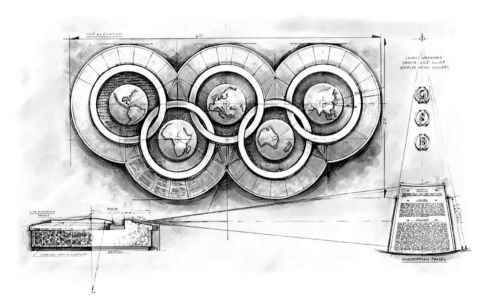

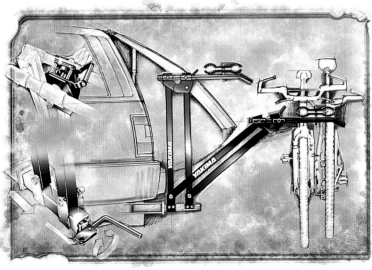

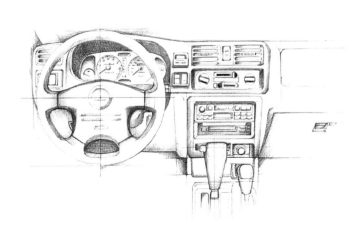

Carol Chislovsky Design, Inc.
853 Broadway, Suite 1201
New York, New York 10003
(212) 677-9100
FAX: (212) 353-0954

CHISLOVSKY

LARRY MOORE Illustrator

Carol Chislovsky Design, Inc.
53 Broadway, Suite 1201
New York, New York 10003
(212) 677-9100
FAX: (212) 353-0954

CHISLOVSKY

SANDRA SHAP — Illustrator

NOBEE KANAYAMA — Illustrator

see
ART

www.showcase.com

Linda de Moreta Represents
(510) 769-1421
FAX: (510) 521-1674

Representing
Peter McDonnell

Nestlé's, Ziff-Davis, Air Touch, Chevron, DHL, Hewlett-Packard, Sega, Pacific Bell, Seagrams, Lewis Galoob Toys

David Goldman Agency
41 Union Square West
Suite 918
New York, New York 10003
(212) 807-6627
FAX: (212) 463-8175
http://idt.net/~dgagency

Norm Bendell

Yes! We have a great animation reel.
Online Samples/Stock Available:
www.sisstock.com Additional samples:
American Showcases 16-20, Directory
of Illustration-Volumes 13 & 14.

Bendell's warm, friendly, sophisticated
style consistently scores very high in
focus groups. Recent clients include:
English Leather/McCabe & Co.,
EMI/In-House, Red Lobster/Grey,
Winterthur (Japan)/PMC-NY,
Novartis/ Earle, Palmer Brown, New
York Times/In-House.

David Goldman Agency
41 Union Square West
Suite 918
New York, New York 10003
(212) 807-6627
FAX: (212) 463-8175
http://idt.net/~dgagency

Norm Bendell

Yes! We have a great animation reel.
Online Samples/Stock Available:
www.sisstock.com Additional samples:
American Showcases 16-20, Directory
of Illustration-Volumes 13 & 14.

Bendell's warm, friendly, sophisticated
style consistently scores very high in
focus groups. Recent clients include:
English Leather/McCabe & Co.,
EMI/In-House, Red Lobster/Grey,
Winterthur (Japan)/PMC-NY,
Novartis/ Earle, Palmer Brown, New
York Times/In-House.

David Goldman Agency
41 Union Square West
Suite 918
New York, New York 10003
(212) 807-6627
FAX: (212) 463-8175
http://idt.net/~dgagency

James Yang

Digital execution of art is available.
Online Samples/Stock Available:
www.sisstock.com

Additional Samples:
American Showcases 16-20, (CD-
ROM Vol. 20) Corporate Showcases
11-13, Directory of Illustrations 12-14,
Creative Options 1 & 2,
Plus numerous award books/annuals.

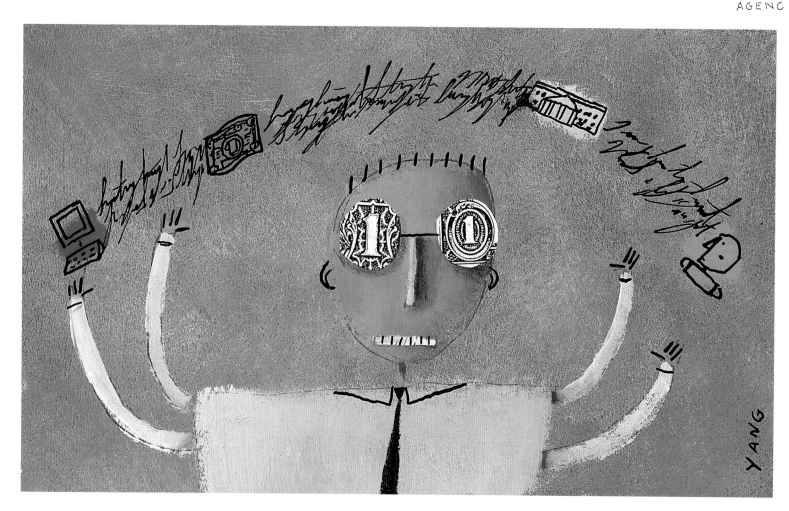

avid Goldman Agency
1 Union Square West
uite 918
lew York, New York 10003
212) 807-6627
AX: (212) 463-8175
ttp://idt.net/~dgagency

James Yang

Digital execution of art is available.
Online Samples/Stock Available:
www.sisstock.com

Additional Samples:
American Showcases 16-20, (CD-
ROM Vol. 20) Corporate Showcases
11-13, Directory of Illustrations 12-14,
Creative Options 1 & 2,
Plus numerous award books/annuals.

David Goldman Agency
41 Union Square West
Suite 918
New York, New York 10003
(212) 807-6627
FAX: (212) 463-8175
http://idt.net/~dgagency

Steve Dininno

Online Samples/Stock Available:
www.sisstock.com

Additional Samples:
American Showcases 16-20 (CD-ROM
Vol. 20), Corporate Showcases 11-13,
Directory of Illustrations 12-14,
Creative Options 1 & 2.

David Goldman Agency
1 Union Square West
Suite 918
New York, New York 10003
(212) 807-6627
FAX: (212) 463-8175
http://idt.net/~dgagency

Steve Dininno

Online Samples/Stock Available:
www.sisstock.com

Additional Samples:
American Showcases 16-20 (CD-ROM
Vol. 20), Corporate Showcases 11-13,
Directory of Illustrations 12-14,
Creative Options 1 & 2.

David Goldman Agency
41 Union Square West
Suite 918
New York, New York 10003
(212) 807-6627
FAX: (212) 463-8175
http://idt.net/~dgagency

Kurt Vargo

Online Samples/Stock Available:
www.sisstock.com

Additional Samples:
American Showcases 15-18, 20 (CD-ROM Vol.20), American Illustration 8, 9, & 11, Directory of Illustration Vol. 13 & 14. Rabbit Ears Titles: "The Five Chinese Brothers" and "The Tiger & The Brahmin".

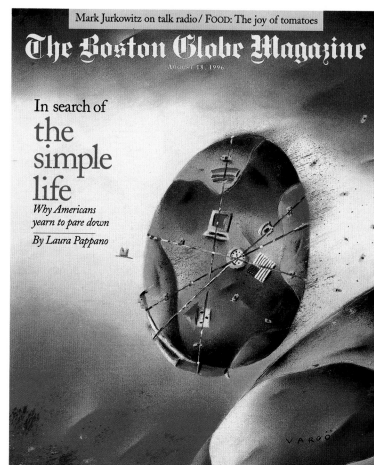

David Goldman Agency

1 Union Square West
Suite 918
New York, New York 10003
(212) 807-6627
FAX: (212) 463-8175
http://idt.net/~dgagency

Kurt Vargo

Online Samples/Stock Available:
www.sisstock.com

Additional Samples:
American Showcases 15-18, 20 (CD-ROM Vol.20), American Illustration 8, 9, & 11, Directory of Illustration Vol. 13 & 14. Rabbit Ears Titles: "The Five Chinese Brothers" and "The Tiger & The Brahmin".

DAVID
GOLDMAN
AGENCY

David Goldman Agency
41 Union Square West
Suite 918
New York, New York 10003
(212) 807-6627
FAX: (212) 463-8175
http://idt.net/~dgagency

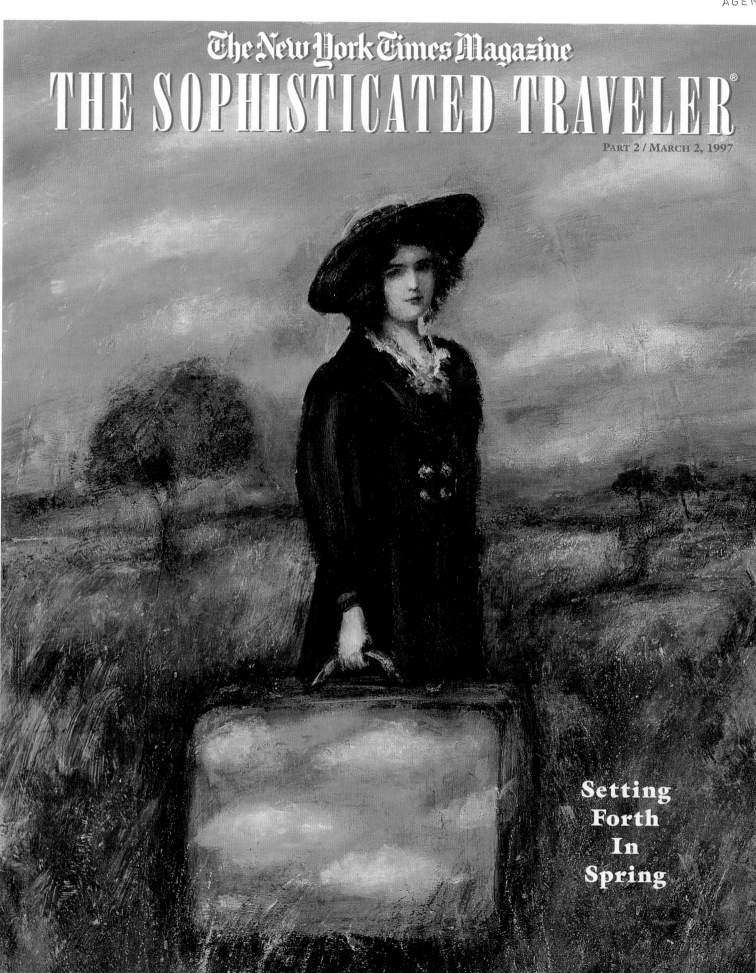

The New York Times Magazine

THE SOPHISTICATED TRAVELER

PART 2 / MARCH 2, 1997

Setting
Forth
In
Spring

David Goldman Agency
1 Union Square West
Suite 918
New York, New York 10003
(212) 807-6627
FAX: (212) 463-8175
http://idt.net/~dgagency

Nishan Akgulian

Online Samples/Stock Available:
www.sisstock.com

Additional Samples:
American Showcases 18-20,
Corporate Showcase Vol. 13,
Creative Options 1 & 2, and
Directory of Illustrations 12-14.

David Goldman Agency
41 Union Square West
Suite 918
New York, New York 10003
(212) 807-6627
FAX: (212) 463-8175
http://idt.net/~dgagency

Kazushige Nitta
Online Samples/Stock Available:
www.sisstock.com.
Specialty Areas Include: Highly
Graphic/Conceptual Work For
Corporate & Editorial Assignments,
and Children's Books/Subjects.

Additional Samples:
American Showcases 15-20,
Corporate Showcase Vol. 13,
Creative Options 1 & 2,
Directory of Illustration Vol. 13, and
Society of Illustrators Vols. 33 & 34.

David Goldman Agency
1 Union Square West
Suite 918
New York, New York 10003
(212) 807-6627
FAX: (212) 463-8175
http://idt.net/~dgagency

Rosemary Fox

Additional Samples:
American Showcases Vols. 17-20.

Specialty Areas Include:
Borders (thematic/high detailed),
Stationery, Book Covers, Original Font
Design, Menus, Children's Subjects.

**Barbara Gordon
Associates**
165 East 32nd Street
New York, New York 10016
(212) 686-3514

Representing:
Bill James

**Barbara Gordon
Associates**
165 East 32nd Street
New York, New York 10016
(212) 686-3514

Representing:
John Suh

**Barbara Gordon
Associates**
165 East 32nd Street
New York, New York 10016
(212) 686-3514

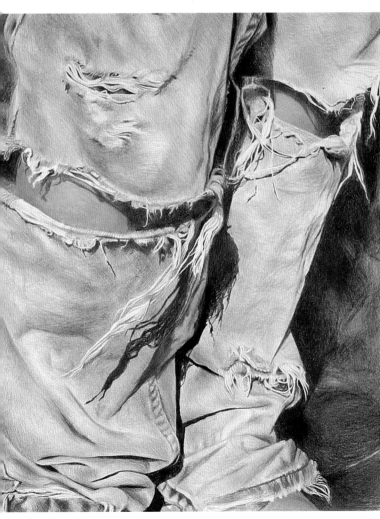

**Barbara Gordon
Associates**
165 East 32nd Street
New York, New York 10016
(212) 686-3514

Representing:
David Elliott

Barbara Gordon
Associates Ltd.
165 East 32 Street
New York, N.Y. 10016
212-686-3514

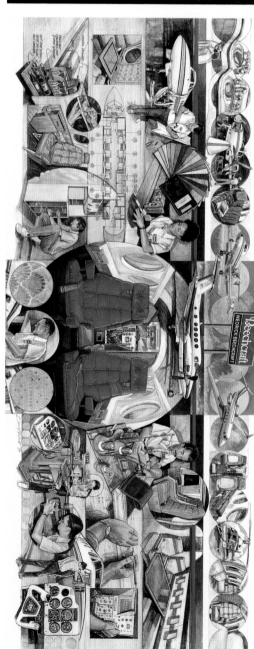

**Barbara Gordon
Associates**
165 East 32nd Street
New York, New York 10016
(212) 686-3514

Representing:
Jim Smola

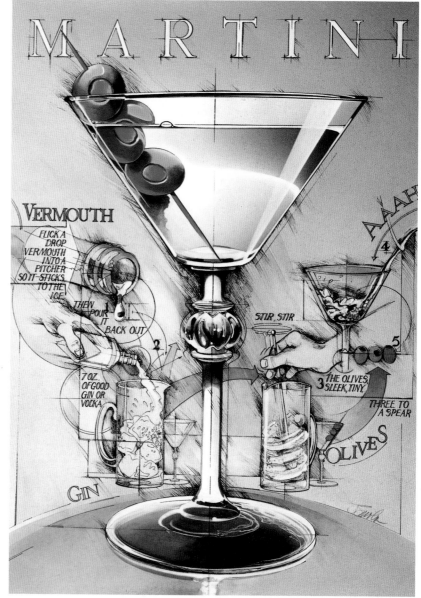

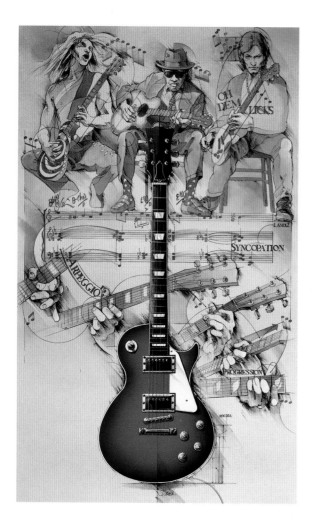

**Barbara Gordon
Associates**
165 East 32nd Street
New York, New York 10016
(212) 686-3514

Representing:
Wendy Christensen

ILLUSTRATIONS FROM DADDY DAY, DAUGHTER DAY • BY LARRY KING & CHAIA KING

see
ART

www.showcase.com

Anita Grien
55 East 38th Street
New York, New York 10016
(212) 697-6170
FAX: (212) 697-6177
agrien@aol.com

Julie Johnson
Represented by Anita Grien

Client include: A&E, Showtime, L'Oreal, Revlon, Macy's, Carnival Cruises, MCI, NYNEX, Texaco, Guinness, Ogilvy & Mather, Saatchi & Saatchi, Avon Books, Rodale Press, Doubleday, Simon & Schuster, The Walt Disney Company.

DENNIS OCHSNER

See.Workbook, Volumes 16, 18, 20

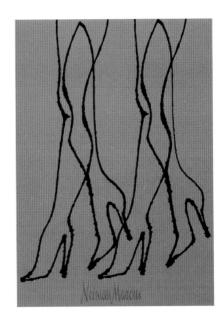

thirst is ...

From the Coca-Cola Annual Report

LAURIE ROSENWALD

REPRESENTED BY PAT HACKETT   Ph 206-447-1600   Fx 206-447-0739   http://www.pathackett.com

Jim Hanson
Artist Agent
(312) 337-7770
FAX: (312) 337-7112
email: jh@jimhanson.com

Representing:
Craig Smallish

Barb Hauser
Another Girl Rep
(415) 647-5660

Web Walk With Barb
http://www.well.com/user/girlrep

Paul Kratter

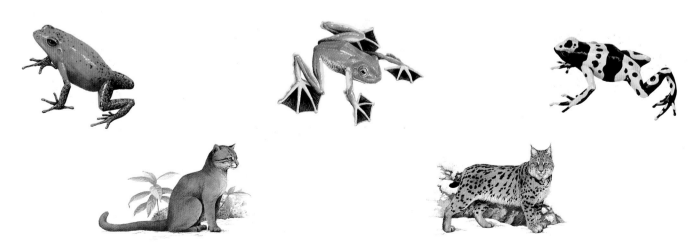

Barb Hauser
Another Girl Rep
(415) 647-5660

Web Walk With Barb
http://www.well.com/user/girlrep

Ben Perini

Ben Perini *i*llustration.

Authentic Illustration.

Barb Hauser
Another Girl Rep
(415) 647-5660

Web Walk With Barb
http://www.well.com/user/girlrep

Miro Salazar

Capital Guaranty

Edison Park

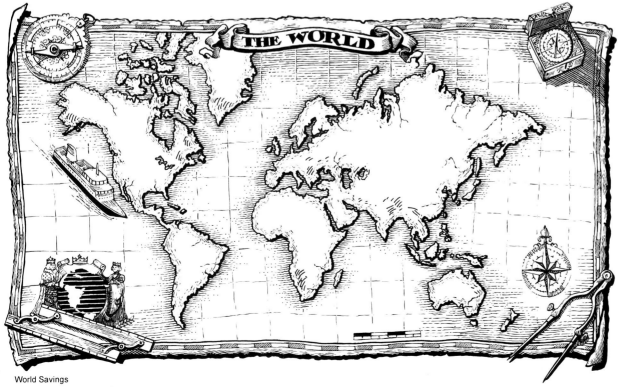

World Savings

Visa

see
ART
www.showcase.com

Suzy Johnston
Artists' Representative
(416) 285-8905
FAX: (416) 285-1509

Clockwise from the top:
ATI Technologies Inc.,
Compaq, Bell Canada
& Evora

MIR
LADA

Suzy Johnston
Artists' Representative
(416) 285-8905
FAX: (416) 285-1509

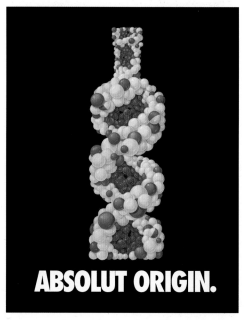

ABSOLUT ORIGIN.

Suzy Johnston
Artists' Representative
(416) 285-8905
FAX: (416) 285-1509

ANSON
LIAW

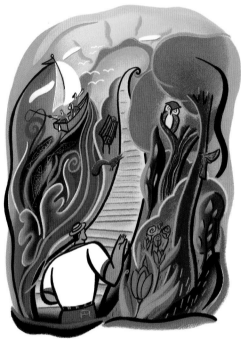

see
ART
www.showcase.com

Tania Kimche
37 Fifth Avenue, 11th Floor
New York, New York 10010
(212) 529-3556
FAX: (212) 353-0831

To view additional work, please see
Workbook Volumes 9-20.

We have a large selection of paintings
available for purchase or secondary
usage.

RAFAL OLBINSKI

MERRILL LYNCH

CIPSCO INC. ANNUAL REPORT

FANNIE MAE

AMERICAN AIRLINES

T A N I A

TANIA KIMCHE ARTIST REPRESENTATIVE

(212) 529-3556 / FAX (212) 353-0831

Tania Kimche
137 Fifth Avenue, 11th Floor
New York, New York 10010
(212) 529-3556
FAX: (212) 353-0831

To view additional work, please see
Workbook Volumes 18-20.

We have a large selection of paintings
available for purchase or secondary
usage.

KEN McMILLAN

HOSHINO U.S.A.

LORD, DENTSU & PARTNERS

CAHNER'S PUBLISHING

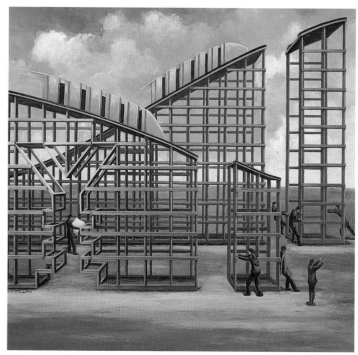

CREDIT SUISSE FIRST BOSTON

ania Kimche
37 Fifth Avenue, 11th Floor
New York, New York 10010
212) 529-3556
AX: (212) 353-0831

West Coast:
Corey Graham
(415) 956-4750

To view additional work, please see
Workbook Volumes 16-20.

K I R K   C A L D W E L L

E.D.S.

THE CONFERENCE BOARD

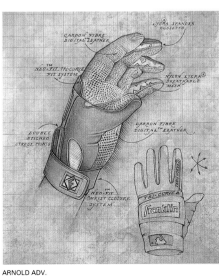

ARNOLD ADV.

CHRONICLE BOOKS

CHAFFIN ADV. CONSTRUCTION

Kirchoff / Wohlberg, Inc.
866 United Nations Plaza
New York, New York 10017
(212) 644-2020

NICOLE RUTTEN

MARNI BACKER

DEBORAH DESAIX

Kirchoff / Wohlberg, Inc.
866 United Nations Plaza
New York, New York 10017
(212) 644-2020

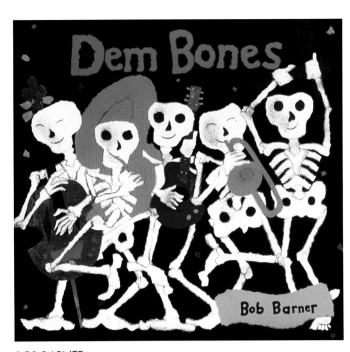

BOB BARNER

MICHAEL GREJNIEC

JOUNG UN KIM

ANDREA WALLACE

Alan Lynch
Artists Representative
(908) 813-8718
FAX: (908) 813-0076

Janet Woolley
Arena

Ian Lynch
Artists Representative
(908) 813-8718
FAX: (908) 813-0076

Elizabeth Harbour
Brigid Collins
Arena

ELIZABETH HARBOUR

ELIZABETH HARBOUR

BRIGID COLLINS

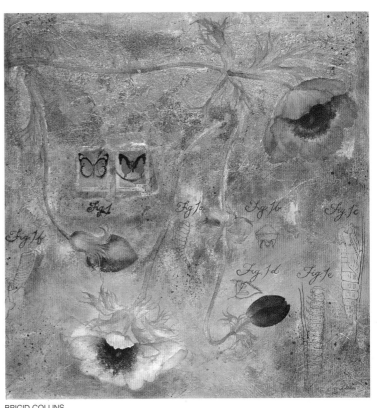

BRIGID COLLINS

Meiklejohn Illustration
28 Shelton Street
Covent Garden
London WC2H 9HP, U.K.
011 44 171 240 2077
FAX: 011 44 171 836 0199

MEIKLEJOHN

MATT EASTWOOD

Meiklejohn Illustration
8 Shelton Street
Covent Garden
London WC2H 9HP, U.K.
011 44 171 240 2077
FAX: 011 44 171 836 0199

Meiklejohn represents over sixty of
Europe's leading illustrators. Call or fax
us to arrange the immediate despatch
of a comprehensive brochure or New
York based portfolios.

MEIKLEJOHN

J AKE RICKWOOD

see
ART

The Neis Group
P. O. Box 174
11440 Oak Drive
Shelbyville, Michigan 49344
(616) 672-5756
FAX: (616) 672-5757

Erika LeBarre
Additional work can be seen in
American Showcase Vol. 19 and 20.
The images below were reproduced by
Zondervan Publishing House, Inc. a
division of Harper Collins, Inc.

Visit our web-site to see additional
work by Erika and others.
My e-mail address is:
neisgrp@accn.org
Partial client list: AAA, Amway Corp.;
Cahners Publishing, Inc.; Chevrolet,
Inc.; Chrysler, Inc.; Coca Cola, Inc.;
Consumers Energy, Inc.; Frontier

Communication Services, Inc.;
G.M.A.C.; Georgia Pacific, Inc.;
Hanley Wood, Inc.; Little Caesar's;
MacMillan/MacGraw Hill; Meijer, Inc.;
Michcon; P.G.A.; Golf Magazine;
Rich's Products Corp.; U.A.W.; and
Zondervan Publishing House, Inc.

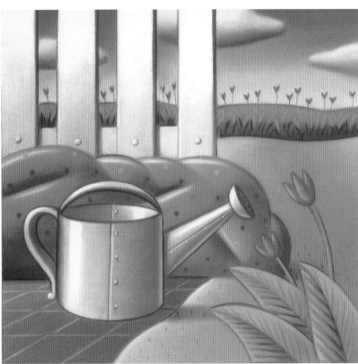

ERIKA LeBARRE
I L L U S T R A T I O N

THE NEIS GROUP
ILLUSTRATION • DESIGN • PHOTOGRAPHY
11440 OAK DRIVE • P.O. BOX 174 • SHELBYVILLE, MICHIGAN 49344-9625
TELEPHONE 616-672-5756 • FAX 616-672-5757 • www.neisgroup.com

The Neis Group
P. O. Box 174
11440 Oak Drive
Shelbyville, Michigan 49344
(616) 672-5756
FAX: (616) 672-5757

Rainey Kirk
Additional work can be seen in American Showcase Vol. 15 thru Vol. 20 including American Showcase CD Vol. 19, as well as the Neis Group website, address below.

Partial client list includes: A.C. Delco; Amway Corporation; B.A. Pargh Co. Inc.; Beck/Arnly World Parts; Bissell Corp.; Bridgestone Corp.; Durango Boots, Inc.; GA Pacific; Holt, Rinehart & Winston; James River Corp.; K.F.C.; Kellogg's, Inc.; Nissan Motor Mfg.; Office Depot; Outboard Marine Corp.; Shoney's, Inc.; Upjohn Co.

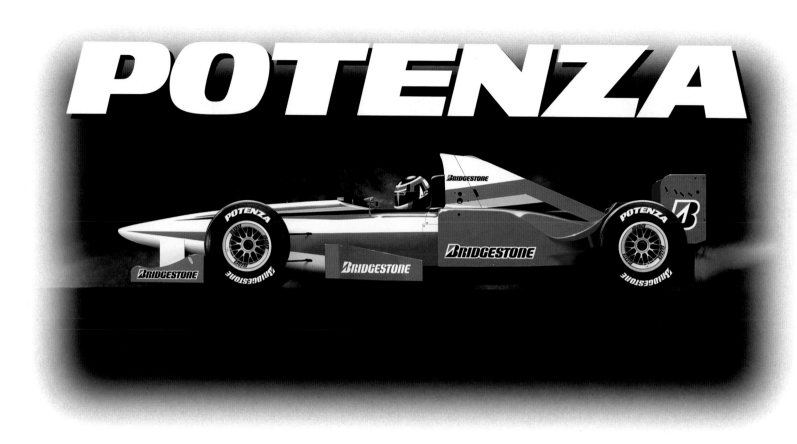

The ultimate racing tires are in the ultimate race.

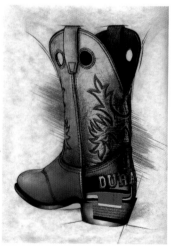
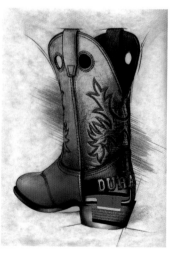

RAINEY KIRK
I L L U S T R A T I O N

THE NEIS GROUP
ILLUSTRATION • DESIGN • PHOTOGRAPHY
11440 OAK DRIVE • P.O. BOX 174 • SHELBYVILLE, MICHIGAN 49344-9625
TELEPHONE 616-672-5756 • FAX 616-672-5757 • www.neisgroup.com

T O M   B O O K W A L T E R
I L L U S T R A T I O N

T H E   N E I S   G R O U P
ILLUSTRATION • DESIGN • PHOTOGRAPHY
11440 OAK DRIVE • P.O. BOX 174 • SHELBYVILLE, MICHIGAN 49344-9625
TELEPHONE 616-672-5756 • FAX 616-672-5757 • www.neisgroup.com

The Neis Group
P. O. Box 174
11440 Oak Drive
Shelbyville, Michigan 49344
(616) 672-5756
FAX: (616) 672-5757

Don McLean
Additional work can be seen in American Showcase Vol. 19 and on the Neis Group website address below.

Partial client list includes: Anheuser-Busch, Inc.; Bell South; Brach's Candy; CBSFox; Chevrolet; Chrysler/Plymouth; Coca Cola, Inc.; Detroit Red Wings; Dr. Pepper; Ford Motor Co.; General Motors; Georgia Pacific, Inc.; Guinness Ale; Hardee's, Inc.; Little Caesar's; Sherwin Williams; Westin Hotels and Zondervan Publishing, Inc.

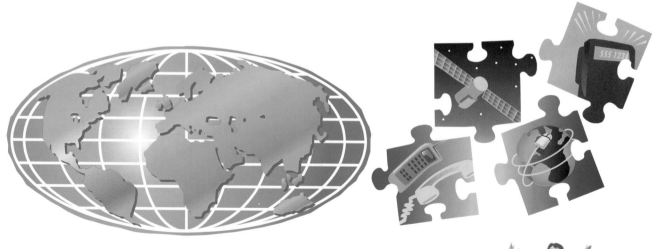

D O N   M c L E A N
I L L U S T R A T I O N

T H E   N E I S   G R O U P
ILLUSTRATION • DESIGN • PHOTOGRAPHY
11440 OAK DRIVE • P.O. BOX 174 • SHELBYVILLE, MICHIGAN 49344-9625
TELEPHONE 616-672-5756 • FAX 616-672-5757 • www.neisgroup.com

The Neis Group
P. O. Box 174
11440 Oak Drive
Shelbyville, Michigan 49344
(616) 672-5756
FAX: (616) 672-5757

Matt LeBarre
Additional work can be seen on the Neis Group website address below.

MATT LᴇBARRE
ILLUSTRATION

THE NEIS GROUP
ILLUSTRATION • DESIGN • PHOTOGRAPHY
11440 OAK DRIVE • P.O. BOX 174 • SHELBYVILLE, MICHIGAN 49344-9625
TELEPHONE 616-672-5756 • FAX 616-672-5757 • www.neisgroup.com

The Penny & Stermer Group
19 Stuy Oval
New York, New York 10009
(212) 505-9342
FAX: (212) 505-1844

Representing
Steve Ellis

West of the Mississippi
Christine Prapas
(503) 658-7070
FAX: (503) 658-3960
Studio
(310) 374-7558
FAX: (310) 318-9079

Please see previous Showcase and Black Book Illustration pages

The Penny & Stermer Group
9 Stuy Oval
New York, New York 10009
(212) 505-9342
FAX: (212) 505-1844

Representing
Rick Stromoski

Please see previous Showcase &
Directory of Illustration for additional
samples.

Rick Stromoski

Represented by The Penny & Stermer Group
For a portfolio review, client list and rates call Carol Lee @ 212.505.9342
Rick's humorous illustrations have appeared in national magazines, children's books,
advertising, licensed products, newspaper syndication and network television.

Vicki Prentice Associates Inc.
630 Fifth Avenue, 20th Floor
Rockefeller Center
New York, NY 10111
(212) 332-3460
FAX: (212) 332-3401

Representing:
Tom Voss
Additional work:
showcase.com

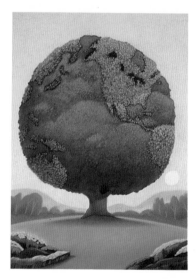

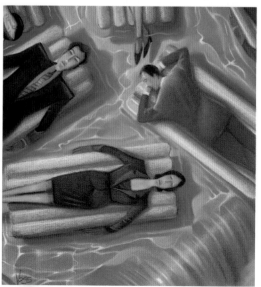

Ravenhill
Helen Ravenhill
(816) 333-0744
FAX: (816) 333-0745

Representing:
Steve Skelton

Ravenhill
Helen Ravenhill
(816) 333-0744
FAX: (816) 333-0745

Representing:
Sandy Appleoff

Also see Workbook 16, 17, 18, 19, 20

Ravenhill
Helen Ravenhill
(816) 333-0744
FAX: (816) 333-0745

Representing:
C.B. Mordan

Also see
American Showcase #20
Workbook #20

SARAH EISLER
REPRESENTED BY

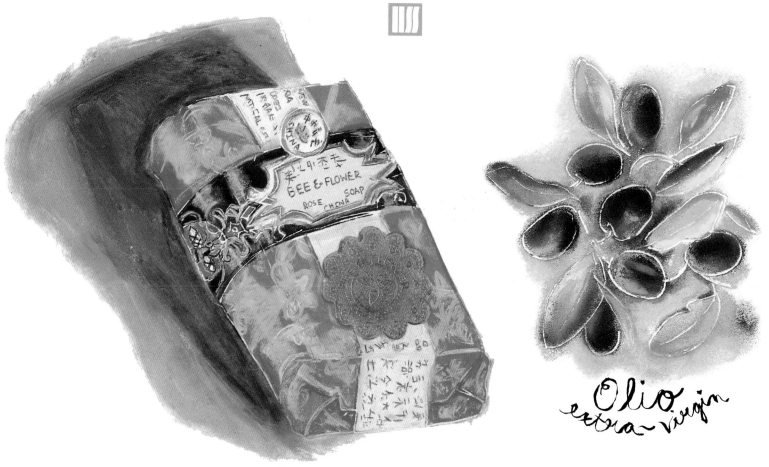

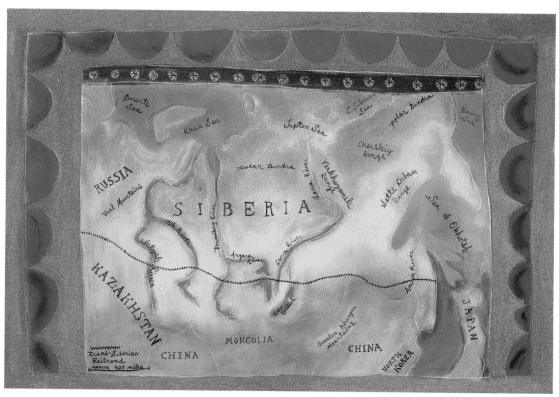

DOROTHY REINHARDT

REPRESENTED BY

JOHANNA HANTEL
REPRESENTED BY

CHRIS LENSCH
REPRESENTED BY

MARK SHAVER

REPRESENTED BY

JOHNEE BEE
REPRESENTED BY

LIZ SANDERS AGENCY
TELEPHONE: (714) 495-3664 FACSIMILE: (714) 495-0129

CLEMENTE BOTELHO
REPRESENTED BY

LIZ SANDERS AGENCY
TELEPHONE: (714) 495-3664 FACSIMILE: (714) 495-0129

AMY NING
REPRESENTED BY

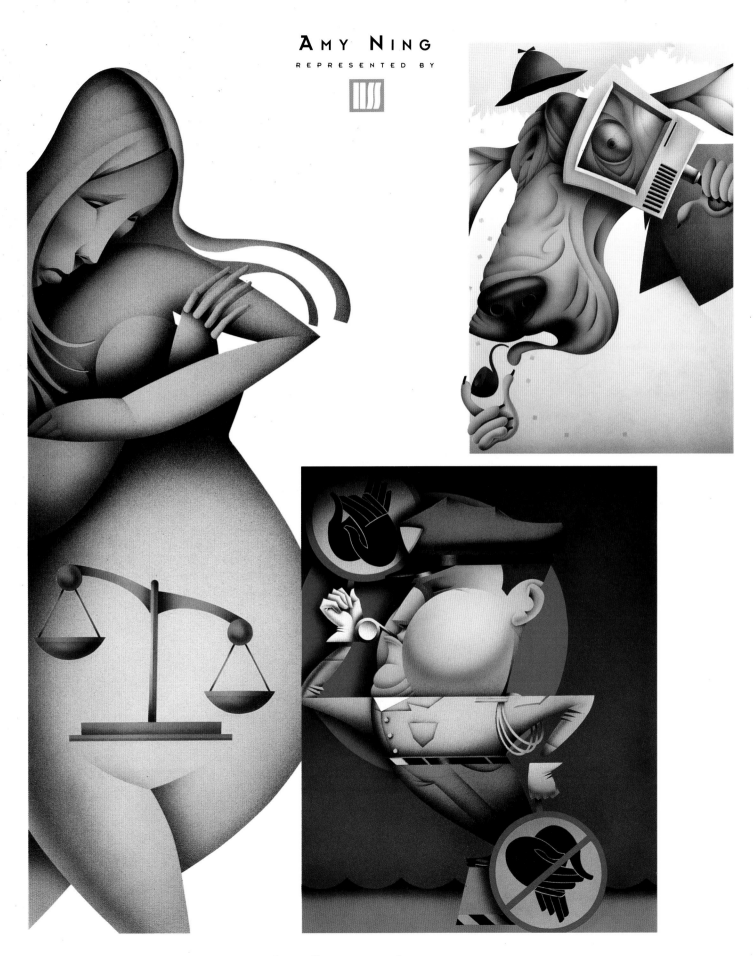

LIZ SANDERS AGENCY
TELEPHONE: (714) 495-3664 FACSIMILE: (714) 495-0129

BACHRUN LOMELE
REPRESENTED BY

CAMERON WASSON

REPRESENTED BY

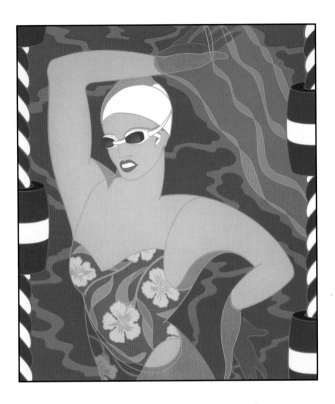

LIZ SANDERS AGENCY
TELEPHONE: (714) 495-3664 FACSIMILE: (714) 495-0129

LARRY DAY

THE MAN WITH THE GOLDEN ARM / NELSON ALGREN

Christina A. Tugeau
Represents:

JAMES BERNARDIN

THE TREASURE ON BESSLEDORF HILL / ALADDIN

THE LEGEND OF THE CANDY CANE / ZONDERVAN

LITTLE FOLKS / HARCOURT BRACE AND COMPANY

CHRISTINA A. TUGEAU

ARTIST AGENT / (203) 438-7307

index

index

index

index

index

index

index

COMPING IS USAGE. ASK FIRST.

see
ART

www.showcase.com